HOSTING

the

PRESENCE

DESTINY IMAGE BOOKS BY BILL JOHNSON

A Life of Miracles

Dreaming With God

Center of the Universe

Momentum

Release the Power of Jesus

Strengthen Yourself in the Lord

The Supernatural Power of a Transformed Mind

Hosting the Presence

Bill Johnson

HOSTING

the

PRESENCE

❖

Unveiling Heaven's Agenda

❖

DESTINY IMAGE₀ PUBLISHERS, INC.
P.O. Box 310, Shippensburg, PA 17257-0310
"Promoting Inspired Lives."

This book and all other Destiny Image, Revival Press, MercyPlace, Fresh Bread, Destiny Image Fiction, and Treasure House books are available at Christian bookstores and distributors worldwide.

For a U.S. bookstore nearest you, call 1-800-722-6774.
For more information on foreign distributors, call 717-532-3040.
Reach us on the Internet: www.destinyimage.com.

ISBN 13 TP: 978-0-7684-0364-0

For Worldwide Distribution, Printed in the U.S.A.

1 2 3 4 5 6 7 8 / 17 16 15 14 13

CONTENTS

Note From Author

USING THE CURRICULUM

It is an honor to come alongside you in what is truly the ultimate quest—to host the Presence of the Lord. The following pages will assist you in this journey.

First, this workbook provides you with interactive group sessions that we will go through together. Additionally, you will have five daily devotional exercises. This is not intended to give you busywork, adding to what you are already doing. The quest to host His Presence is a great privilege and delight, not religious duty.

In these daily exercises you will honestly engage the questions that follow each of the entries. As you go through each one, yielded to the Holy Spirit's direction and dependent upon His instruction, you will go from "glory to glory" in your relationship with the Lord and will be transformed all the more into a vessel that hosts His Presence and impacts your world.

You will engage in additional study by doing daily Bible readings, using some of the key Scriptures from this curriculum, along with reading short daily segments in the *Hosting the Presence* book (these are the HTP readings at the end of each daily devotional).

As you bend your heart toward pursuing Him, your hunger for His Presence, power, and glory will increase daily. May the following study stir an unquenchable thirst within you to host the most incredible

Person on the planet, the Holy Spirit, and see the world around you changed because of *Christ in you* being released.

INTRODUCTION

I am amazed at the momentum created by the woman who reached out to touch the hem of Jesus' garment. What began as a single, radical touch shifted into a testimony, positioning others with sickness and affliction to recognize that they too could experience Jesus' healing power through touching His clothing.

Wherever He entered villages, or cities, or countryside, they were laying the sick in the market places, and imploring Him that they might just touch the fringe of His cloak; and as many as touched it were being cured (Mark 6:56 NASB).

In Mark 5:25-34, we read the testimony of this woman's supernatural healing. In the following chapter, we witness the ripple effect of this bold act of faith. Her testimony produced an expectation in the people—that by touching Jesus' clothing, they could be healed. This explains why the masses thronged Jesus, imploring that they might "just touch the fringe of His cloak." Were they correct? The results don't lie: "as many as touched it were being cured." Touched what? The fringe of Jesus' cloak.

The question begs: Was there something supernatural about Jesus' clothes?

Fast forward to the Book of Acts. There was still an expectation that physical contact with an anointed item would release the miraculous. In Acts 19:11, we read about the "extraordinary miracles" (NASB) performed by Paul. There was even a shift in miracles, from works to the "greater works" Jesus introduced in John 14:12, as evidenced by this new class of miracles given the title *extraordinary*. Remember, the woman with the issue of blood came to Jesus. But with Paul, people were taking pieces of his clothes to the sick and using them as points of contact to release healing and deliverance.

In both cases, with Jesus and with Paul, the release of power had little to do with an item or piece of clothing. The woman with the issue of blood was not placing her faith in the hem of a garment, but rather in the One wearing the garment. Likewise, people were not placing their confidence in the power of Paul's clothes, per se. It was the Presence on and in Jesus that made the garment powerful, just as it was the Presence upon Paul that made him a powerful Kingdom ambassador and Christ representative. The same is true for you!

You might be wondering, "What does it mean to host God's Presence? As a believer, I thought God's Presence—the Holy Spirit—lived inside of me already. Is there a difference between being filled with the Spirit and hosting His Presence?" Let me put it this way: If you were renting a house from me, I wouldn't walk into the home without an invitation, or at least without your permission. Though the house belongs to me and I am renting it to you, I am not going to barge in, ruffle through the refrigerator, and start cooking a meal for myself. Why? Although it is legally my house, it is under your charge and stewardship.

The Holy Spirit indwells every believer. The question is, how many believers are actually stewarding His Presence well?

Works and greater works, miracles and extraordinary miracles—these are the expression of a lifestyle that hosts God's Presence. Our job? Treat the One who possesses our lives as the honored Guest. He won't force His way in. Rather, He desires redeemed humanity to co-labor with Him out of a place of intimacy in order to bring His purposes to fruition on the planet.

Few are aware of this assignment to host God; even fewer have said *yes*. I believe you will be among the few and represent King Jesus well in your generation.

Bill Johnson
Bethel Church

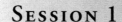

SESSION 1

YOUR AUTHORITY TO RELEASE GOD'S PRESENCE

To become world changers, it is important that we first recognize the authority we have received and exercise it in our own lives to experience breakthrough. It cannot be a concept or teaching; it must be the reality we walk in as normal Christianity! We have been freely given God's Presence so that we could freely release it.

"God called and positioned mankind to be the delegated authority over the planet."

—BILL JOHNSON

11

VIDEO GUIDE

1. Jesus restored the keys of _____ to humanity and commissioned us to go.

2. Since God's original design and plan, _Sin_ had entered the world.

3. Since Jesus has all authority, the devil has _NO_ authority.

4. God called and positioned mankind to be the _Kingdom_ authority over the planet.

5. God is raising up a company of people to bring divine _miracles_ back to the planet.

6. Jesus performed His miracles as a _man_, not as God.

Day 1

RULING AUTHORITY

…But only speak a word, and my servant will be healed. For I also am a man under authority, having soldiers under me. And I say to this one, "Go," and he goes; and to another, "Come," and he comes; and to my servant, "Do this," and he does it.

—MATTHEW 8:8-9

While the earth always belonged to God, man and woman—Adam and Eve—were given a very unique assignment. They were delegated to be the ones who ruled planet earth in God's name, under His authority. Scripture makes it clear that God possesses and owns the planet (see Ps. 24:1), but He has given the assignment of rulership to the "sons of men" (Ps. 115:16 NASB).

Though sin entered the equation and humanity poorly stewarded this authority, the truth is that this mandate has not been withdrawn or retracted. It is mankind's created function. You were created to rule and exercise Kingdom authority. The key to successfully stewarding this authority has everything to do with our willingness to be under God's rule.

Matthew 8:5-13 reveals a clear example of this authority structure in action. The Roman military leader realized that his authority came from being under the authority of a superior. From the beginning, that was God's master design. Remember, God created everything and ultimately owns it all. He is our Ruler. Man and woman were granted authority over the earth because they were designed to rule in the nature and likeness of God.

We can only release the benefit of God's rule flowing out of us to the degree that His rule is over us. God does not release Kingdom authority to and through rebels. Conversely, by demonstrating a grasp of this type of authority structure, the Roman official is actually applauded by Jesus, for he reveals a clear understanding of the supernatural origin of this authority structure. May we do likewise in our Christian lives.

- Daily Reading: *HTP*, Pages 31-33

- Daily Scriptures: Matthew 8:5-13, Genesis 1:26, 2:9, Psalm 24:1, Psalm 115:16

QUESTIONS:

(For Questions 1 and 2, read Matthew 8:5-13)

1. What does Jesus specifically commend the Roman centurion for?

   For his faith in believing that all Jesus had to do was speak and the servant would be healed. He knew the authority

2. What do you think the connection is between the centurion's understanding of authority and his faith in the healing word of Jesus?

   He was a man of authority as well + he could recognise the authority Jesus has.

3. List three areas in your life that you need to submit to God's authority and rulership:

    a. _My entire walk_

    b. _My healing_

    c. _My marriage_

4. What do you learn about God's established authority structure by reading Psalm 24:1 and Psalm 115:16?

    a. The heavens belong to the _Lord_

    b. The earth has been given to _man_

Day 2

THE UNHIDDEN AGENDA: TO SUBDUE THE EARTH

Then God blessed them, and God said to them, "Be fruitful and multiply; fill the earth and subdue it; have dominion over the fish of the sea, over the birds of the air, and over every living thing that moves on the earth."

—GENESIS 1:28

Adam and Eve were given a unique mandate in the Garden. In addition to tending their immediate environment in Eden, they were instructed to *subdue* the earth. This implies a forceful, militant subjugation. Of what? The darkness on the outskirts. There was a world of chaos and darkness beyond the Garden. Satan had fallen from heaven and was cast down to planet earth (see Isa. 14:12; Rev. 12:4). There was perfection—the Garden of Eden—but beyond its borders was a planet that needed what mankind provided: divine authority.

The Garden was God's model for the climate and culture that He desired to fill the earth with. Before God gave mankind the commandment to subdue, they were instructed to *"be fruitful and multiply"* (Gen. 1:28). The structure of this passage is very intentional. In the beginning, Eden could adequately

17

house Adam and Eve. But once they started to have more and more children, it would become a tight fit. The offspring of the first man and woman were God's solution to the darkness that was just beyond Eden's borders.

For the first man, the commission was to bring everything outside of the model (Eden) into subjection to the model. To successfully reproduce the culture of Eden in the dark, chaotic regions of a desolate planet, it only makes sense that mankind's mandate would include subduing the earth.

Just as man's authority has not been revoked, you too are commissioned to subdue everything in your life that is in opposition to God's perfect model—Jesus. God created order in the midst of disorder so that those made in His image might represent Him well by extending the borders of the Garden of Eden until the whole planet would be covered with God's rule *through* His delegated ones. The same is true for you!

- Daily Reading: *HTP,* pages: 33-34

- Daily Scriptures: Genesis 1:26-28, Revelation 12:4

QUESTIONS:

1. What was God's commission to man in the Garden? (Gen. 1:26-28)

    a. To be *fruitful* and *multiply*

    b. To *fill* the Earth.

    c. And *subdue* it (the Earth).

2. Why would God give Adam and Eve instructions to subdue the Earth?

He wanted the Garden of Eden to spread outside
+ cover the earth.

3. What are some areas where God wants you to fulfill this same commission through your life?

a. Areas that God wants to speak strength and courage to:

Going to church regular + becoming involved
in ministry. Get back to preaching His truth.

b. Areas where you experience weakness, but God is calling you to bring the Kingdom:

Reaching out to others. Walk through the
doors that God opens with power + boldness

Day 3

WARRING FROM VICTORY

And they heard the sound of the Lord God walking in the garden in the cool of the day, and Adam and his wife hid themselves from the presence of the Lord God among the trees of the garden.

—GENESIS 3:8

In the Garden, Adam was not given any tools—teaching or training manuals on spiritual warfare. He simply walked in the cool of the day with the Lord. Obviously, the threat of darkness was real and near, as a chaotic world existed just outside of Eden. Satan had now entered the equation. How was mankind expected to subdue darkness and fill the planet with God's government? It was to happen through intimacy.

Kingdom dominion was established through relationship with the King. Emphasis was not on principles, but on a person. Relationship was prized above all else, for humanity was meant to rule *out of* relationship, and, in turn, exercise authority over darkness *out of* relationship. When we know who He is, what He's like, and what life is like in His world, by default the things that conflict and disagree with Him are the very things that must be subdued.

21

This is not a call to spiritually careless living. Paul admonishes us in Second Corinthians 2:11 not to be *ignorant* of the devil's *schemes*. Spiritual warfare is a reality that believers need to appropriately engage in. Overemphasis on it, however, is just as unhealthy as ignorance. In the Garden of Eden, satan was not the focus because mankind had not yet sinned and granted him authority. And the same should be true for us today—after the Cross, satan should not be the focus because he is a defeated foe.

From the moment mankind fell, God was not taken off guard. Satan is crushed under the feet of man. The Anointed Man, Jesus, won the victory, and ever since His resurrection, anointed men and women throughout the ages have been granted the same position of victory over the serpent. We do not war for victory, as if it were up to our methods and works to obtain it. Rather we war *from* victory. We war *from* a position of intimacy with the Ultimate Victor, and are enforcing the victory He has already purchased.

- Daily Reading: *HTP,* Pages 35-36

- Daily Scriptures: Gen. 3:1-16, 2 Cor. 2:11

QUESTIONS:

1. *Who* and *what* was the main focus in the Garden of Eden?

   God + intimacy with Him was the main focus.
   Adam was given dominion + was to subdue it.

2. What do you think it means to war *from victory* versus warring *for victory*? How is spiritual warfare different for you if you believe Jesus has already defeated the enemy, instead of thinking that you have to do something in order to win this victory?

We war from victory because with Christ we already
won the battle.

With Jesus, He has already fought all of our battles.
Without Him, we are fighting against ourselves.

3. How does your relationship with God actually position you to confront and subdue the enemy?

My relationship with God positions me to confront
& subdue the enemy because through intimacy with
Him gives me that right.

Day 4

POSSESSING WHAT OUR MATURITY CAN MANAGE

And the Lord your God will drive out those nations before you little by little; you will be unable

to destroy them at once, lest the beasts of the field become too numerous for you.

—DEUTERONOMY 7:22

When it comes to filling the earth with God's glory by exercising Kingdom authority, this mandate has been extended to all believers throughout all generations. No exclusions. Why, then, does it seem like so many Christians live in defeat rather than victory? It has everything to do with maturity. Simply put, some believers are unable to step into new levels of victory and authority, not because of God's unwillingness to give it, but because greater privilege could potentially destroy the ill-prepared and immature.

Contrary to legalistic belief, maturity is not having everything together and walking in absolute perfection; instead, it begins with a posture or bend of the heart. Those qualified to possess God's promises are those with hearts bent toward His Presence and glory. If the ultimate aim is self-promotion rather than seeing God's glory fill the earth and Jesus' name being exalted, there is still some heart work that needs to be done.

Adam and Eve's extension of authority and possession in Eden paralleled what Israel was to experience later in possessing the Promised Land. God had given Israel the entire Promised Land. It belonged to them all at once, and it was their inheritance by promise. However, they possessed only what they had the ability to manage and steward well.

God lovingly restrains us from possessing the fullness of our inheritance and destiny, not because He wills to withhold it, but because His will is life and preservation. If God granted us access to possess the fullness of our inheritance *now*, it would most likely destroy us. It is our possession by grace and grace alone. But no gracious God would give His children something that would overwhelm and destroy them.

---

* Daily Reading: *HTP*, Pages 36-38

* Daily Scriptures: Deuteronomy 7:17-24, Exodus 23:29-33

QUESTIONS:

1. List four things you believe that God has promised you, that you are still waiting to receive:

   a. _____

   b. _____

   c. _____

   d. _____

2. As each of these promises comes to pass, how do you see the demonstration of God's glory, through Him entrusting you with increase and fulfillment, in these areas?

   a. _____

b. _____

c. _____

d. _____

3. Why do you think God gives people access to possessions "little by little," instead of all at once? (Example: Israel and the Promised Land in Exodus 23:30.)

_____

_____

_____

_____

_____

JESUS—HIS MODEL AND MANDATE BELONG TO YOU

So Jesus said to them again, "Peace to you! As the Father has sent Me, I also send you." And when He had said this, He breathed on them, and said to them, "Receive the Holy Spirit."

—JOHN 20:21-22

Jesus set aside His divine privileges and lived as a man anointed by the Holy Spirit. In turn, His humanity qualified Him to be both Messiah and model. He purchased back the keys of authority from satan as the God-Man, and, through His years of public ministry, He modeled to believers throughout the ages what the normal Christian life would look like. He served as the model because He was the Anointed Man.

Even though Jesus was 100 percent God during His time on earth, He chose to do ministry as one anointed by the same Holy Spirit that you and I received at salvation. What does this mean for us? Since we have received this same Spirit that raised Jesus from the dead, God has made powerlessness inexcusable and unacceptable (see Rom. 8:11).

By default, Jesus' model reinforces our mandate. What is this mandate? Simple: John 20:21. In the same manner the Father sent Jesus, Jesus is now sending us. What is He sending us to do? Matthew 10:7-8 states:

> And as you go, preach, saying, "The kingdom of heaven is at hand." Heal the sick, cleanse the lepers, raise the dead, cast out demons. Freely you have received, freely give.

When Jesus breathed upon the disciples in John 20:22, He was basically saying to them, "What you have watched Me do—this is *your* mandate. Go and do the same things!" Jesus' ministry was their model and His breath (the Holy Spirit) was their empowerment. Remember, Jesus was dependent upon the Father when it came to what He *did*. Likewise, as the Father sent Jesus to *imitate* a model, so Jesus has anointed and commissioned you and me to do the same. We are to imitate and represent Jesus. To represent Jesus, we literally are *re*-presenting Him to the world.

* Daily Reading: *None*

* Daily Scriptures: Matthew 10:7-8, John 20:21-22

QUESTIONS:

1. What does it mean that Jesus set aside His divine privileges and lived as a man who was anointed by the Holy Spirit?

_____

_____

_____

_____

2. According to John 20:21 and Matthew 10:7-8, what are believers commissioned to do?

3. According to John 20:22, what empowerment does Jesus give us to fulfill this commission?

4. If Jesus worked miracles, not because He was God, but because He was a man anointed by the Holy Spirit, what does this mean for your life as one called to imitate Jesus and do what He did?

Session 2

YOUR SIGNIFICANCE IN HIS PRESENCE

Before we are positioned to release God's Presence to the world and impact our spheres of influence, it is vital that we recognize our significance as believers. We are filled with His Presence and minister in His Presence. Because of Jesus' work, we are priests unto God. We minister directly to Him, in His Presence. It is out of that place that we are empowered to minister in the "outer courts" to people, both in the church and in the world.

"When you discover who God has made you to be, you will never want to be anyone else."

—BILL JOHNSON

VIDEO GUIDE

1. In redemption, we are restored to an identity _____ than before the Fall.

2. The enemy enters our lives through _____.

3. We _____ the liar through our agreement with his lies.

4. We have been called by God to be _____ unto the Lord.

5. Two ministries of priests:

   a. To _____.

   b. To _____.

6. Two ministries to people:

   a. To _____.

   b. To the _____.

7. We always _____ like whatever we worship.

8. Thanksgiving is our response to God's _____.

9. Praise is focused on God's _____.

10. In worship, we are the _____.

Day 1

GOD'S ANSWER MAY JUST BE...YOU!

So God heard their groaning, and God remembered His covenant with Abraham, with Isaac, and with Jacob. And God looked upon the children of Israel, and God acknowledged them.
—Exodus 2:24-25

Cries and fervent prayers have been offered throughout the generations for a historic move of God's Spirit. Interestingly enough, the answer typically comes in the package of a person. Looking back through the halls of history, God has anointed men and women to be revivalists, reformers, and agents of transformation in their respective generations.

Beginning with Moses, we observe God's tendency to answer prayers using people. In Exodus 2, we note that God hears the groaning of His people who were in bondage to the Egyptians at the time. He is a covenant-keeping God. It is not merely something God does, but it is who He is, etched into the very fabric of His nature. His heart is to deliver, restore, and revive. How does He do this? Through ordinary people who are filled with the Presence of someone extraordinary and otherworldly.

It is important that we are clear on this. People, in and of themselves, are not able to provide, let alone *be* the answer to cries for deliverance and revival. In and of ourselves, we possess nothing and, in turn, offer nothing of substance to hurting humanity. The reality that we must come to terms with is that *we are not alone*. If you are born again, you are filled with God. He is the answer. He is the solution. He alone can satisfy the generational cries for reformation, revival, and renewal. This is where you and I factor into the equation.

He does not reside in a temple of sand and stone. God's home is not buildings; it is people. He lives in people, so that through people He can accomplish the impossible and use men and women as His anointed agents to *be* the answers the earth is groaning for.

---

* Daily Reading: *HTP*, Pages 49-52

* Daily Scriptures: Exodus 2:15-25, 2 Samuel 5:1-12

QUESTIONS:

1. How did God ultimately use Moses as the answer to the cries of Israel?

_____

_____

_____

_____

_____

2. Read Second Samuel 5:1-12. How did God use King David as the answer to Israel?

_____

_____

_____

_____

3. Can you think of other men or women in the Bible whom God raised up in response to the cries and prayers of His people?

_____

_____

_____

_____

4. What does the following statement mean to you: "You are uniquely positioned in this world because of the cry of other people" (Bill Johnson)?

_____

_____

_____

_____

Day 2

FACE TO FACE WITH GOD

But since then there has not arisen in Israel a prophet like Moses, whom the Lord knew face to face...

—DEUTERONOMY 34:10

There are two incorrect ways we can read passages like Deuteronomy 34:10. The first way is by looking back, and the second way is by looking forward. Let me explain.

Under the Old Covenant, Moses enjoyed encounters with God that were, by and large, unparalleled. Not many had the privilege of beholding the Lord "face to face," experiencing His glory and goodness to the degree that Moses did. One way to respond to the reality of Moses' face-to-face relationship with God is to simply commemorate what *was* in the past. "Well, that *was* Moses. He *was* an Old Testament deliverer, prophet, and an all-around, extremely important guy." We memorialize encounters like Moses' and distance them from the grasp of our present-day experience. "That *was* then...this is now."

Secondly, there is looking forward to the "day" when we all experience God in a face-to-face manner. Again, Moses' experience with God is still disconnected from present-day reality, and does nothing to make us hunger for a now-encounter with the God of Glory. Why? Because we cannot hunger for what is beyond reality and availability. If knowing God face to face, like Moses did, comes when we get to heaven, then there is no point in hungering for an experiential relationship with Him here on earth, since it is inaccessible *until* that day.

However, both perspectives are incorrect. Moses serves as a prototype for what would become available to every single believer. Even the apostle Paul recognizes that the "ministry of the Spirit" comes with increasing glory than what was even experienced in Moses' day (see 2 Cor. 3:7-11). The Presence that Moses encountered actually lives inside of you and positions you to enjoy a face-to-face relationship with God Almighty. It is time to start expecting superior things from a superior covenant!

- Daily Reading: *HTP*, Pages 52-54, 58-59

- Daily Scriptures: Deuteronomy 34:10, 2 Corinthians 3

QUESTIONS:

In view of Deuteronomy 34:10:

1. What does it mean to memorialize face-to-face encounters with God, distancing them from our current experience?

_____

_____

_____

_____

2. What does it mean to put an experiential, powerful relationship with God off to the future?

_____

_____

_____

_____

3. Read Second Corinthians 3. Based on what the apostle Paul is writing to the Corinthian church, what kind of relationship with God and experience with His glory is available to *you*—a New Covenant believer?

_____

_____

_____

_____

Day 3

NOT DESIGNED TO MAKE
YOUR HEAD BIGGER

And God spoke to Moses and said to him: "I am the Lord. I appeared to Abraham, to Isaac, and to Jacob, as God Almighty, but by My name Lord I was not known to them."

—Exodus 6:2-3

God revealed Himself to Moses in a way that not even Abraham, the father of our faith, had received. Likewise, God has revealed Himself to you and me in a way that no Old Testament patriarch had ever experienced. They only received previews, foretastes, and glimpses of what you and I now freely enjoy.

Think about it. What you enjoy with God as the "norm" is something our faith forefathers burned to merely catch a glimpse of (think of Moses yearning to simply catch a glimpse of God's glory in the cleft of the rock). Now, since we have been born again and filled with the Holy Spirit, does this grant us permission to settle and become comfortable with where we are in our relationship with God, *or* does it stir within us an insatiable hunger to pursue and experience as much of His glory this side of heaven as possible?

The way into the Kingdom is narrow. In fact, there is only one way and His name is Jesus. That said, it is false advertising for us to insinuate that life *within* the Kingdom is narrow. Far from it. It is large, vast, and infinite. There are no limits for the believer who has resolved in their hearts to pursue the fullness of His Presence *on earth*.

Revelation of what is accessible inside of this massive Kingdom is not intended to increase our understanding of theological concepts. Revelation precedes new levels of relationship. What we experience in our encounters with God becomes the benchmark for what we realize we offer the planet. Since we are filled with the encountering Presence of God, by default you and I are walking, talking encounters with God, just waiting to collide with lost, hurting, and broken people who need to know He is good.

---

* Daily Reading: *HTP*, Pages 53-54

* Daily Scriptures: Exodus 6:2-3, Ephesians 3:14-19

QUESTIONS:

1. How does the new way that God revealed Himself to Moses impact their relationship? (See Exodus 6:2-3, and how God revealed Himself to Abraham, Isaac, and Jacob as *God Almighty*, but now was revealing Himself to Moses as *the Lord*.)

---

2. How does the new way God has revealed Himself to you change the way you relate to Him? (This "new way" is what Jesus provided, making a way for the Holy Spirit to live inside of you—see Hebrews 10:20.)

_____

_____

_____

_____

3. If the Presence of God lives inside of you, how does this transform the way you interact with people—*what do you have to offer them?*

_____

_____

_____

_____

Day 4

THE SUPERNATURAL POWER
OF GOD'S PRESENCE

And you shall be to Me a kingdom of priests and a holy nation.

—EXODUS 19:6

Exodus 19:6 was fulfilled through Jesus, who made us kings and priests to our God. Priests minister in the Presence of God. When we look at King David, we see a prototype of a priest ministering before the Lord. He received revelation that God responds to the praises of His people by releasing His Presence.

Is it any wonder that the devil is terrified of a worshipping people? He is not bothered by complacent worship. Such is really an oxymoron. Worship, by the very nature of the word, demands all. This is the type of person who is a true threat to darkness. They are all in. They are not looking to do the bare minimum, hoping to merely "punch the God clock" and move on to real life. His Presence *is* real life. Everything else is extremely secondary.

Darkness is threatened by our worship because we are transformed into the likeness of who we worship, and that likeness is Jesus—someone the enemy does not want to deal with. Now, before the Holy Spirit took up residence within us, the prospect of us actually taking on the likeness of God—the object of our worship—was a stretch. Religion does not have the power to produce supernatural transformation, only temporary modification. For us to truly reflect God and model Jesus in the earth, we need to be possessed with His Presence; and one of the ways the Presence touches and transforms us is through worship.

You can see why worship is such a key factor in our lives. When His indwelling Presence and manifest Presence collide, the atmosphere becomes charged with the climate of heaven. This is how people are healed, delivered, and restored in worship—before anyone even has the opportunity to pray for them! Worship ushers in the government of our homeland. When His Presence comes, His rule and reign follow and touch everything that is in disagreement with His divine order.

- Daily Reading: *HTP*, Pages 54-57

- Daily Scriptures: Psalm 22:3 (KJV), 2 Chronicles 20:14-19, Acts 16:22-30

QUESTIONS:

1. Read Psalm 22:3 in the King James Version of the Bible, along with Second Chronicles 20:14-19. What does it look like for God to inhabit the praises of His people?

_____

_____

_____

2. Can you think of any experiences in God's Presence (at church, by yourself, at an event, etc.), where God moved miraculously for you (or someone else)?

_____

Briefly share your testimony(s):

a. _____

_____

_____

b. _____

_____

_____

c. _____

_____

_____

A Note on Testimony:

It is important to remember and record testimonies where you experienced God's Presence transforming your life or someone else's life. These testimonies possess power. When you remember what God has done, you are building a history with Him that positions you to face the future with confidence, expecting God to powerfully manifest His Presence *again*. He may do it differently, but the very nature of a testimony is an account or story that is told to stir faith and create expectancy that He will do it again!

Day 5

---◆---

A REPUTATION MARKED BY THE PRESENCE

For how then will it be known that Your people and I have found grace in Your sight, except You go with us? So we shall be separate, Your people and I, from all the people who are upon the face of the earth.

—Exodus 33:16

How do you want to be remembered? In Moses' dialogue with God, we see the very element that assigns our significance and defines our reputation—the Presence of God. This distinguishes you from everyone else "upon the face of the earth." Scripture definitely teaches us the value of establishing a good name (see Prov. 22:1). However, too many pursue the wrong things when it comes to legacy and reputation. Beauty and skills ultimately fade. But when you are recognized as a relentless pursuer of His Presence, generations to come will become hungry for God by studying your life and pursuit of the Lord.

Don't *feel* important, significant, or like you are worthy to be one through whom generations are transformed by God's Presence? Excellent. That positions you to be the very person you feel unqualified to be.

Review biblical history and revival history. God specialized in using the unqualified. Why? His Presence is the significance of that person. It is never about them and anything they could naturally do.

God's Presence empowers the weak, lowly, downtrodden, and rejected to be the very agents that go down in history as game changers for the Kingdom.

There was nothing special about Israel, qualifying them to be chosen by the Lord. God's manifest Presence would be their distinguishing mark (see Exod. 33:16). The same was true for a more contemporary example, Kathryn Kuhlman. She was not renowned for being a great Bible teacher, dynamic orator, spectacular singer, or natural beauty. Her significance was totally wrapped up in her identity as one who hosted God's Presence well. Are you willing to take your place in your generation—in your family, your church, your city, and your sphere of influence—and receive the significance that only comes from being a man or woman who pursues and hosts His Presence?

---

* Daily Reading: *HTP*, Pages 59-62

* Daily Scripture: Exodus 33:12-23

QUESTIONS:

1. Can you think of three examples of people in the Bible who were insignificant, and through the empowering Presence of God became history makers? (Tip: A good place to start would be Hebrews 11.)

    a. ....

    b. ....

    c. ....

2. Take these same three people and briefly explain *how* God used them as His agents of transformation.

a. _____

_____

b. _____

_____

c. _____

_____

3. Research some contemporary heroes of the faith (for example: Billy Graham, Kathryn Kuhlman, Smith Wigglesworth, etc.). Be careful to study their lives *before* they became recognizable and notice how God took seemingly insignificant people and transformed them into world changers.

_____

_____

_____

_____

_____

SESSION 3

EMPOWERED BY HIS PRESENCE

Gideon is an Old Testament prototype of what all believers have access to today—the ability to be empowered by God's Presence to accomplish the impossible! Remember, God does not look at our weakness; He looks at our Presence-empowered potential and calls it forth.

"God says, 'I will be with you' because He just gave someone an impossible assignment. The God who invades the impossible is with us."

—BILL JOHNSON

VIDEO GUIDE

1. What you _____ infects what you worship.

2. God has a name for you that is the opposite of your greatest _____.

3. God wants to use your _____ to illustrate His message.

Day 1

EMPOWERED TO RELEASE GREATER GLORY

"The glory of this latter temple shall be greater than the former," says the Lord of hosts.
—Haggai 2:9a

It is wise for us to study the lives, ministries, and exploits of the Old Testament prophets, for they give us a preview of what is available to all believers today. They were truly an unusual group of people, as their encounters with God—particularly through the anointing of His Presence—are often labeled benchmarks for spiritual experience.

These prophets of old were the most feared and respected people in the Old Testament. Kings and rulers consulted them. Nations rose and fell because of the anointed decrees of these otherworldly spokesmen. But what separated them from everyone else on the planet? The very thing that we have received because of the work of Calvary—access to the Presence of God. And to think, what *rested upon* the prophets of old has come to *abide in* us.

Old Covenant theology did not have a concept for the Holy Spirit's home. He rested upon people for certain seasons and to perform specific exploits, but the very thought that God would take up residence within humanity *and remain* was not part of the paradigm.

Sadly, many believers today are living under an Old Covenant paradigm without even knowing it. The Spirit lives within them, yes, but He is not hosted and released through their lives. The activity of the prophets should give us a preview of the effect that the Presence should produce in our lives.

Though the Spirit did not permanently abide in the prophets of old, they actually stewarded the anointing more effectively than many do today. How? The Spirit rested upon them, and they moved. They spoke. They obeyed. They pursued. They performed the miraculous. They healed the sick. They raised the dead. Their prayers and decrees transformed nations and revealed God's very nature to the onlooking world.

Remember, the prophets existed in the days of the *former house*. You and I are in the age of the *latter house*. In fact, we *are* the latter house—full of glory!

---

* Daily Reading: *HTP*, Pages 65-67

* Daily Scripture: Haggai 2:1-9

QUESTIONS:

1. How has Jesus made greater glory accessible to us than what was even experienced in the Old Testament?

_____

_____

_____

_____

2. List three prophets from the Old Testament who quickly come to mind. What were the results of their encounters with God's Presence? (What did they *do?*)

a. _____

_____

b. _____

_____

c. _____

_____

3. What does it mean to steward the Presence of the Holy Spirit?

_____

_____

_____

_____

Day 2

EMPOWERED BY PEOPLE OF PRESENCE

Then the Spirit of the Lord will come upon you, and you will prophesy with them and be turned into another man.

—1 SAMUEL 10:6

God was setting King Saul up for a transforming experience in His Presence. Let's put aside everything Saul did wrong for a moment and simply study his divine encounter and how it changed him "into another man."

Saul was given specific instructions on where to go for his supernatural setup. He was told to go where the other prophets were prophesying, and there he would be changed. The Spirit of God was already moving in that atmosphere, so when Saul approached them, what was already on the prophets came upon Saul.

The Spirit of God resting upon a person, and specifically manifesting through that individual, should create a hunger within us for a similar encounter with the Presence of the Lord.

Sadly, failure and imperfection have sabotaged this experience for many. Our propensity is to look at anointed individuals and get hung up by their flaws. When we see the flaws, or worse, when their

61

failures become clear, loud, and public, we completely write off their anointing. In fact, the tendency is to discount it, identify it as demonic in origin, and/or want nothing to do with it.

Obviously, Saul did not end well. We do not by any means skirt over his sin and failure. However, just as we learn valuable lessons from other flawed heroes of the Bible, we must also recognize the activity and Presence of the Lord upon those who finish both positively and poorly. The key is always stewarding the anointing well. Saul failed here, but you and I have the opportunity to draw from God's Presence to cultivate a lifestyle of power and purity, and stir future generations to hunger for what we had without stumbling over our failures. Gifts are free, but maturity is expensive.

- Daily Reading: *HTP*, Pages 71-72

- Daily Scripture: 1 Samuel 10:1-13

QUESTIONS:

1. What does the following statement mean to you: "Gifts are free, but maturity is expensive"? How does this relate to your empowerment by the Holy Spirit?

_____

_____

_____

_____

2. In First Samuel 10:1-13, we read about King Saul's transforming encounter with God through his experience with a group of prophets. Have you ever been in an environment (church service,

conference, camp, etc.) where God's Spirit was moving, and because of what He was doing in other people, you were encouraged to pursue God with greater passion and hunger? Describe this experience.

_____

_____

_____

_____

3. List three individuals in Scripture who experienced some type of major failure (sin, moral failure, idolatry, etc.) in their lives, but who God still used mightily.

a. _____

b. _____

c. _____

Day 3

EMPOWERED WITH POTENTIAL

…As the Father has sent Me, I also send you.

—JOHN 20:21

King Saul had a powerful encounter in God's Presence, as many have enjoyed throughout the ages. How is it, then, that people can experience a life-changing touch from His Presence and seemingly "turn back?" Simple. God initiates encounters, but He is not responsible for our potential. We are. He designs us with built-in potential, absolutely. The key is stewarding it, and this comes by recognizing Jesus' model.

As believers, we are filled with the most significant potential imaginable—the empowering Presence of God lives inside of us! All of heaven has been assigned to ensure that we have everything we need to reach our God-designed destinies. What is the key? Activity.

Not works or religious activity. Remember, we did nothing to earn or deserve the infilling of His Presence. This was released to us completely by grace. Too many are working for what they have already received by inheritance and thus live perpetually frustrated. This often positions believers to ask for things that are already theirs. Rather than asking, we ought to be decreeing what the Lord has already declared as "so."

God is not looking for activity, in the religious sense. We are not working for Him, but are rather co-laboring with Him. We recognize what activity we should be "doing" when we intimately confront the Jesus of the Gospels. Not the Jesus of religion, nor the Jesus of tradition. We need to have a deep, transformative encounter with Jesus, as He is, for He has sent us in the same manner the Father sent Him (see John 20:21).

We must work with the Holy Spirit to fulfill our potential and actually live what Jesus paid for us to experience as the normal Christian life. When we look at Him, we come face to face with the will of God for every Presence-filled believer: *re*-presenting Jesus!

---

* Daily Reading: *HTP*, Pages 72-74

* Daily Scriptures: Matthew 10:1-15, John 20:19-23

QUESTIONS:

1. Based on Matthew 10:7-8, what are Jesus' instructions to His disciples?

_____

_____

_____

_____

2. How do these verses answer the question: "What is God's will for my life?"

_____

_____

_____

_____

3. Since the Holy Spirit lives inside of you, you possess the potential to do the same works Jesus did. List some of the works that Jesus did during His earthly ministry.

a. _____

b. _____

c. _____

d. _____

Note: Jesus' works reveal what the normal Christian life should look like.

Day 4

———◆———

EMPOWERED TO MAKE A DIFFERENCE

Gideon said to Him, "O my lord, if the Lord is with us, why then has all this happened to us? And where are all His miracles which our fathers told us about, saying, 'Did not the Lord bring us up from Egypt?'"

—JUDGES 6:13

When Gideon encounters the angel of the Lord, he asks an age-old question that people are still hung up on today: "If God is with us, why has all this bad stuff happened? And where are the miracles we have always heard about?" It is amazing how quickly we make the bad stuff God's "sovereign will." It is a sad day when we point our fingers at God, accusing Him of being less than good, rather than actually evaluating ourselves and asking, "Where have we possibly missed it?"

Gideon asked a question that so many of us want answers to. God's response? For one, it was not, "Gideon, I decided to withdraw My miraculous power from the earth for a season so I could teach My people a lesson by giving them trials, tribulations, and afflictions." Many mistakenly believe God holds out on providing a miracle because He has some spiritual lesson that He wants to teach us by prolonging our suffering.

We are not promised a life without adversity. We are certainly not guaranteed a persecution-free existence. That said, when it comes to sickness, torment, fear, bondage, oppression, addiction, and all of the like, we have been instructed to represent Jesus and destroy the works of the devil (see Acts 10:38).

Often, we are awaiting some sovereign solution to the madness and chaos in life, when, in fact, God's Word to us is the same as it was to Gideon: "Go in this might of yours....Have I not sent you?" (Judg. 6:14). Gideon was one of those Old Testament figures who were empowered by the Spirit for a task and a season. You and I have received the abiding Presence of the Holy Spirit. Our lives are His home and that positions us to always be ready to go in "this might" (which is God's supernatural strength), and release whatever a situation, circumstance, or impossibility needs for transformation.

---

* Daily Reading: *HTP*, Pages 76-77

* Daily Scripture: Judges 6:11-14

QUESTIONS:

1. Many believers are waiting around for God to provide a sovereign solution to problems, when His instruction to us is simple: "Go!" How does this change the way you respond to the circumstances that you face in life?

---

2. In Judges 6:13, Gideon asked the Angel of the Lord, "…If the Lord is with us, why then has all this happened to us? And where are all His miracles which our fathers told us about…." How can constantly sharing testimonies of the works, signs, and wonders God performs actually stir spiritual hunger in a generation yet to be born?

Day 5

EMPOWERED TO BE ENCOURAGED
IN UNLIKELY PLACES

"But if you are afraid to go down, go down to the camp with Purah your servant, and you shall hear what they say; and afterward your hands shall be strengthened to go down against the camp." Then he went down with Purah his servant to the outpost of the armed men who were in the camp.

—Judges 7:10-11

What holds many of us back from taking our place in the Kingdom and being people who make a difference? Fear. We received the commission. We had the encounter. We know the Word and are filled with the Presence. But still, we face fear head-on.

Let's look at Gideon for a moment. He was also afraid when things got started and he stepped out to take his place as a reformer in his generation. In fact, we see that he is still afraid in the middle of the story. Just because we take a step of faith does not mean fear ceases its attack. Often, it intensifies the further we move toward God's purposes. Surely, it didn't help much when God decided to reduce Gideon's army from 32,000 down to 300!

What did God instruct Gideon to do to deal with his fear? Something that only makes sense in God's paradigm: "Go down to the enemy's camp." The reasoning is simple. In the enemy's camp—in the world plagued by impossibility, defeat, hopelessness, atrocity, war, terminal illness, discouragement, and depression—we are given a glimpse of the very elements that heaven longs to powerfully overthrow through us.

Everything in the enemy's camp is contrary to God's government. These things are absent in His world, correct? Well, if our model truly is *on earth as it is in heaven,* and we observe things in this world that clearly have been perverted and assaulted by the enemy, we should receive encouragement. Why? Because these broken things are being set up for God's ambassadors—you and me—to release His Kingdom and usher in His perfect will. Gideon was given a unique vision of the enemy's camp. When he journeyed down there, he eavesdropped on a fearful adversary, for the enemy was having dreams of Gideon wiping them out. Make no mistake, the powers of darkness tremble because they recognize that the fight is fixed. What, or more specifically, Who you carry is what trumps their efforts every time!

- Daily Reading: *HTP,* Page 78

- Daily Scripture: Judges 7:9-25

QUESTIONS:

1. How do you face impossible situations with the awareness that God is fighting for you? (Examples: A confrontational work environment; unbelieving family members, peers, neighbors, colleagues, and classmates, etc.)

---

2. Gideon was called by God to do what was counterintuitive to his fear: Go down to the enemy's camp. By facing this, Gideon discovered God's victory in the midst of darkness. What situations or personal fears do you feel God is asking you to face? Ask Him what His perspective is and how He wants to bring His Kingdom into those situations.

A SNEAK PREVIEW OF GOD'S HOUSE

Jacob received a prophetic blueprint for the normal Christian life in Genesis 28. Jesus was the initial fulfillment and model, but He ultimately pointed to the Presence-empowered community of believers—the Church—as the house of God, the fulfillment of Jacob's dream. Such is characterized by an open heaven, the voice of God, and a continuous flow of supernatural/angelic activity from one world to the other.

"The Lord has built His house on the edge of two worlds."

—BILL JOHNSON

VIDEO GUIDE

1. The house of God has:

   a. An open _____ .

   b. _____ activity.

   c. The _____ of God.

2. A gate is a _____ place from one realm to another.

3. God has built His house on the edge of _____ worlds.

4. Jesus becomes _____ _____ of the house of God prophesied in the Old Testament.

5. Earth invaded heaven _____ heaven invaded earth.

Day 1

---※---

GOD CONCEALS TO REVEAL

It is the glory of God to conceal a matter, but the glory of kings to search out a matter.
—PROVERBS 25:2

When it comes to deciphering God's will and becoming acquainted with His ways, we must change our thinking. Many of us consider God's ways as mysteries beyond the grasp of man. We think that if God decides to let us in on what He wants to do (or what He currently is doing), then great. Otherwise, we live out our lives in a perpetual waiting room, not expecting, but only wishing and hoping that God reveals what He wants, when He wants to.

I repeat: we must change the way we think when it comes to receiving answers from heaven. In the Kingdom, things are hidden *to be found*, not to be concealed and remain mysterious. Jesus Himself stated, "…It has been given to you to know the mysteries of the kingdom of heaven…" (Matt. 13:11).

Why does God hide things from us and yet extend an invitation to search them out? Simple. The answer is so that we discover truth, revelation, discernment, understanding, direction, and answers. The "things" we are searching for cannot become our ultimate quest, even though they are often godly in nature. He must be our pursuit. He conceals in order to reveal. The key is that God does not just intend to give us what we need, but out of relationship and intimacy with us, He wants to share His heart on the very things we are seeking out. He wants to personally lead us through the process.

After going through this process and obtaining what we have been searching for, we walk away recognizing that the object we pursued would have no meaning or value apart from what His Presence assigns to it. He is our quest. He is the object of our pursuit. He is the One who whispers answers and shares secrets with His people. In conclusion, it is not so much about what we need *from Him,* but it becomes about everything we receive *in Him.* Everything we are searching for is accessible in His Presence!

- Daily Reading: *HTP,* Pages 81-82

- Daily Scriptures: Proverbs 25:2, Matthew 13:10-11

QUESTIONS:

1. Read Matthew 13:10-11 and Luke 8:9-10. Consider what Jesus is saying about our being able to know the mysteries of His Kingdom. How should this truth change your expectation level when you approach God for answers?

   _____

   _____

   _____

   _____

2. What does God want to teach you in the process of receiving answers from Him?

   _____

_____

_____

3. What can happen to your relationship with God if all you seek Him for are answers to prayers (instead of actually discovering the answers *with* Him)?

_____

_____

_____

_____

Day 2

THE DAY OUR FOREFATHERS LONGED TO SEE

…Blessed are the eyes which see the things you see; for I tell you that many prophets and kings have desired to see what you see, and have not seen it, and to hear what you hear, and have not heard it.

—LUKE 10:23-24

Take a moment and think of some of the Old Testament heroes of the faith…who *dreamed*. We think of men like Abraham, Solomon, David, and Daniel. Jesus was speaking of these men (and others), when He was addressing His disciples in Luke 10:23-24. The question we should be asking ourselves is, what did (and would) the eyes of the disciples see, and what would they experience that kings and prophets of old wished to see and experience?

At first, the answer seems simplistic: Jesus, right? Yes, but we need to get a little more specific than that. It is the person of Jesus and the Kingdom that He inaugurated in His earthly ministry. The context of verse 24 is very clearly the disciples doing the works of the Kingdom (in this case, setting people free from demonic torment).

Our faith forefathers looked to the day when mankind would receive a new heart and a new nature, along with an era when the Spirit of God would live inside every believer. This day was and is wrapped up in the person of Jesus. However, it also includes His work and activity. Those who lived under the Old Covenant had a built-in awareness that a superior day was coming. As we consider this reality, I pray we begin to recognize the honor of the day we have been sovereignly stationed in, and begin to draw from the inheritance we have received in the New Covenant.

The patriarchs of old, the prophets, the kings, the judges—these individuals whose experiences with God we consider the zenith of people who enjoyed proximity to His Presence—actually longed for our day! This should make us joyfully reexamine what we have branded the normal Christian life, and start asking the Holy Spirit to show us how to walk in the superior covenant and enjoy everything the Father has reserved for us in this hour.

- Daily Reading: *HTP*, Pages 83-85

- Daily Scripture: Luke 10:17-24

QUESTIONS:

1. When you read that the day in which you live is actually the time that Old Testament heroes looked forward to, what thoughts come to your mind?

_____

_____

_____

2. List some of your Old Testament heroes of the faith:

   a. _____.

   b. _____

   c. _____

   d. _____

3. Consider the great exploits these people performed, or supernatural experiences they enjoyed with God. What enables people today to enjoy the same (if not, greater) encounters with God than what the Old Testament forefathers had?

_____

_____

_____

_____

_____

Day 3

THE INVITATION TO TASTE AND SEE

Oh, taste and see that the Lord is good...

—Psalm 34:8

Have you ever gone to see a movie because the trailer made it look so funny that you couldn't miss it; but when you actually saw it, you noticed all of the funny moments in the movie were already in the trailer? Needless to say, it's a great letdown.

With that in mind, let us contrast the movie example with what a supernatural sneak preview releases. The taste and the preview are always an invitation to something that exceeds, not disappoints. Tastes are open doors to greater, deeper encounters with God.

It is amazing how the Kingdom works contrary to natural order. For example, in the natural world, when we don't eat, we start to get hungry, right? It does not work like that in God's Kingdom. In the Kingdom, we actually get hungry through tasting and eating. Why? Because the One we taste of is so glorious, so great, so large, and so exceedingly beyond anything we could hope, dream, or imagine, that one taste leaves us longing for the more of God that our encounter reveals is available.

Any snapshot we receive of God exposes us to the One who is infinitely beyond our ability to scratch the surface of in this lifetime. Should this fact discourage us? I mean, didn't Jesus come so that we could *know God*? He sure did. We just need to be careful when it comes to defining what this *knowing God* looks like.

Some people assume they know God because they appear to know a lot of theological information. Sadly, information is very different from a personal, intimate, experiential knowledge of God. Information by itself puffs up the head, leaving the heart stale (see 1 Cor. 8:1). Pursuits that are sparked by a taste of His Presence and power, on the other hand, humble us. We realize how little we know about the great God that we serve, and yet recognize how much we are accessible to in His Presence. Worship leader Misty Edwards notes that we will "never exhaust the discovery of God." Aren't you glad?

---

* Daily Reading: *HTP*, Pages 85-86

* Daily Scripture: Psalm 34:8-10

QUESTIONS:

1. What are some practical ways you can "taste and see" that the Lord is good?

_____

_____

_____

_____

2. List some things that have made you hungry to experience more of God.

(Note: It might have been a significant church service, a supernatural encounter, a miracle, an answered prayer, a conference, a missions trip, etc.)

_____

_____

_____

_____

3. What was it about these special moments that caused you to pursue God more passionately?

_____

_____

_____

_____

Day 4

THIS IS YOUR MOMENT!

You know how to discern the face of the sky, but you cannot discern the signs of the times.
—MATTHEW 16:3B

One of the enemy's primary strategies is to make us discount the moment we have been placed in. Why? It sabotages our effectiveness. We must remember that heaven is our destination, but this planet and its people are our present assignment.

We discount our present moment by having a skewed perspective of the past and future. When we believe the past is unsurpassable and that the encounters with God enjoyed by those of yesteryear is the pinnacle and cannot be touched, we will memorialize a former day and spend the present looking back to the "good ole days."

Likewise, when we place too much emphasis on the future, be it end-times speculation or a preoccupation with getting to heaven one day, we can see how we start to devalue our unique moment in history. Surely, when we do this, it is poor stewardship of God's present assignment upon our lives.

Each of us has received an assignment that is intentional and time-specific. Think about it. You and I were not dropped into the days of Moses, Elijah, or Jesus. Likewise, there is a chance that we might not be stationed in the last of the last of the last days of civilization prior to the Lord's return. Does this give us the right to long for the past or yearn for the future, all the while discounting where we are right now? Not at all.

Truth be told, we are living in the most glorious time in history. Remember, as long as we idolize another era, we will be blind to the importance of our own. It is right and good to long for heaven as our home. But it is our responsibility to equally long for His rule here and now. God's job is to get me to heaven. My job is to bring heaven to earth through my prayers and obedience.

- Daily Reading: *None*

- Daily Scripture: Matthew 16:1-4

QUESTIONS:

1. Read Matthew 16:1-4. When Jesus refers to the "signs of the times," in context, what is He specifically talking about?

_____

_____

_____

_____

2. What happens when we value the moment God has strategically placed us in?

_____

_____

_____

....

3. What does the following statement mean to you: "Heaven is my destination, earth is my assign-

   ment" (Bill Johnson)?

_____

_____

_____

_____

Day 5

---◆---

THE GATE OF HEAVEN

How awesome is this place! This is none other than the house of God, and this is the gate of heaven!

—Genesis 28:17

One of the most powerful sneak previews in the whole of Scripture is found in Genesis 28, where Jacob witnesses a heavenly ladder with angels ascending and descending upon it. This account gives us a glimpse of the unrestricted flow of supernatural resources that would become accessible to anyone who would live under an open heaven. Jesus was both the forerunner and the model, which we find in John 1:51 and Luke 3:21-22.

In Luke 3, the heavens broke open at Jesus' baptism—the Holy Spirit was released upon Him—and they have not shut ever since. In John 1, Jesus specifically speaks of His fulfillment of Genesis 28, promising His followers that they would witness the heavens open, and angels ascending and descending upon *the Son of Man*. It is interesting that He specifically identifies Himself as the Son of Man in this instance. This might have been a real paradigm-shifter. For angels to ascend and descend upon the Son of God, that would totally make sense. But for the Son of *Man?* Jesus' baptism commenced His model for the normal Christian life; and this model can only be followed by those living under an open heaven.

How do we do this? It is by stewarding the Presence. You see, the empowering Presence of the Holy Spirit lives inside of you and me. He is the One who positions us to live under an open heaven, just as He did for Jesus—the Son of Man. That title, *Son of Man*, is significant because it refers to His identification with humanity. In other words, the fullness of heaven's supply and resources flow through the person, Presence, and power of the Holy Spirit. Jesus was and is the Eternal God, but He also lived as the Son of Man anointed by the Holy Spirit. This was to show you and me, the sons and daughters of man, how to live under an open heaven and release the resources of heaven into the earth through the Spirit of God.

- Daily Reading: *HTP*, Pages 88-90

- Daily Scriptures: Genesis 28:10-22, Luke 3:21-22, John 1:43-51

QUESTIONS:

1. Read Genesis 28:10-22. What is unusual about Jacob identifying the place where he was as the "house of God"?

Note: This is the first use of the phrase *house of God* in the Bible, so it is essential for us to pay close attention to what is being communicated here in terms of God's original intent and purpose for His house.

2. Read Luke 3:21-22. What did the "open heavens" release into Jesus' life?

_____

_____

_____

_____

3. Read John 1:43-51. Why is it significant that Jesus identifies Himself as the *Son of Man* in reference to supernatural activity (angels ascending and descending) and open heavens?

_____

_____

_____

_____

4. How does this impact your understanding of what is available to you as a Spirit-filled believer?

_____

_____

_____

_____

SESSION 5

THE ANSWER TO ANCIENT CRIES

Isaiah 64:1 expresses the ancient cry of God's people to see Him come down and move in power among them. Because of Jesus, this cry has been fulfilled. He modeled the anointed, Presence-empowered Christian life and then, because of His redemptive work, made a way for every believer to walk under an open heaven—experiencing and releasing the supernatural power of God today!

"The Holy Spirit lives inside of every believer, but does not rest upon every believer."

—BILL JOHNSON

VIDEO GUIDE

1. The Holy Spirit lives inside of every believer, but He does not rest _____ every believer.

2. A key to hosting the Presence of God: take every step with the _____ in mind.

3. When we are _____ of an open heaven, we live differently.

4. Jesus did not live in reaction to darkness; He lived _____ to the Father.

5. There is a difference between what we have in our _____ and what we have in our _____.

6. Every outpouring of the Holy Spirit contains the _____ of God.

Day 1

THE CRY FOR A PERSON

Oh, that You would rend the heavens! That You would come down! That the mountains might shake at Your presence...

—ISAIAH 64:1

I grew up hearing that there was a God-shaped hole in the core of every person. And I still believe it. In fact, one of the passages in Scripture that so clearly displays this cry for divine fulfillment is Isaiah 64:1. The hole, void, or vacuum within every single human being can only be satisfied by one thing—the Presence of God.

Quite literally, God Himself has built us for habitation; hence, this corporate awareness for what is "missing." Cries have been resounding throughout the ages for the very thing Isaiah 64:1 contends for. Specifically, the cry is for the heavens to break open and for God to release a significant Presence into the planet through His people. After all, the Presence being pursued is one that caused mountains to shake. This is not a flutter in our heart or goose bumps during a nice song. Something beautifully violent is portrayed here...and was fulfilled by Jesus at His baptism.

Do you know why Jesus' water baptism was so significant? It inaugurated the model all mankind would be able to follow upon receiving the Holy Spirit. Consider it for a moment. Did Jesus *need* to be baptized? No. He was without sin. His baptism was not a sign of His redemption, but rather illustrative in nature. From the moment He was baptized in water, He was setting the stage for His anointed public ministry. His baptism was a landmark moment that actually began to answer the ancient cries for an open heaven and a powerful unleashing of God's Presence into the earth.

At Jesus' baptism, heaven opened and the Spirit of God descended upon Him. Jesus not only answered the age-old cry for open heavens and released Presence, but the supernatural ministry that followed His baptism provided an example for every single person who would say *yes* to Him, receive His redemptive work, and become filled with the same Spirit that anointed Him for ministry.

- Daily Reading: *HTP*, Pages 93-95

- Daily Scriptures: Isaiah 64:1, Mark 1:10-11, Matthew 3:13-17

QUESTIONS:

1. 1. Read Mark 1:10-11 and Matthew 3:13-17. Why was Jesus baptized by John?

_____

_____

_____

_____

2. How does Jesus fulfill the cry of Isaiah 64:1?

_____

_____

_____

_____

3. If Jesus' baptism was the launch of His earthly ministry, and this ministry is a model for how we should live the Christian life, what does this mean for you as a follower of Jesus now?

_____

_____

_____

_____

Day 2

THE CRY FOR AN OPEN HEAVEN

When He had been baptized, Jesus came up immediately from the water; and behold, the heavens were opened to Him, and He saw the Spirit of God descending like a dove and alighting upon Him.

—MATTHEW 3:16

The language of *open heavens* points to an unrestricted flow of supernatural resources from God's world to this one. The catalyst is always an anointed individual. Jesus was the model for what it looked like to live under an open heaven. He never intended for His experience to be unparalleled or unreachable, as Jesus' earthly ministry is an invitation to us to rise higher in our Christian lives. We need to elevate our expectations for what this thing called discipleship looks like, otherwise, it only makes sense that believers will become bored and burnt out.

Randy Clark notes that many believers actually live a bored, unsatisfied Christian experience, not because of God's unwillingness or inability to do anything, but because of what I call the "closed heaven between the ears" syndrome. They believe the heavens "are as brass" and, therefore, adopt a closed-heaven

Christianity as the norm. This may have passed for a while, but God is graciously awakening His people. Those possessed by the Spirit cannot shake their longing to live under the open heavens Jesus provided.

In fact, Jesus was the initiator of the open heaven reality we are called to live in. This would be impossible without Jesus' example, but above all, without His blood. Jesus' blood and sacrifice on the Cross paid the penalty for our sin so that the power of heaven could take up residence within our hearts in the form of the Holy Spirit.

This means that you are a significant threat to darkness. The key is not allowing the darkness around us to shape our awareness of the Kingdom atmosphere that we carry. Remember, greater is He and the Presence living in you. Now take that revelation to the next level. The greater Presence inside of you was always meant to be released to transform the environment around you!

---

* Daily Reading: *HTP*, Pages 97-98

* Daily Scripture: Matthew 3:16

QUESTIONS:

1. What comes to your mind when you think of the phrase *open heavens*?

----

2. How does being aware of the Holy Spirit's presence upon you affect your perspective of your impact on the darkness around you?

_____

_____

_____

3. How does what you believe about your status in Christ impact the way you live out your Christian life?

_____

_____

_____

4. Can you identify some inaccurate ways of thinking that misrepresented what Christianity has looked like to you?

_____

_____

_____

5. What did this type of thinking do to your walk with the Lord?

_____

_____

_____

Day 3

THE CRY FOR HIS PRESENCE TO COME

In the year that King Uzziah died, I saw the Lord sitting on a throne, high and lifted up, and the train of His robe filled the temple.

—ISAIAH 6:1

"Holy Spirit...come." This invitation has the ability to confound and confuse people, as it raises the question: How can the Holy Spirit come to where He already lives? Yet, countless revivals, supernatural encounters, and moves of God have been sparked by that simple invitation for the Holy Spirit to show up and move in power. The key to navigating this properly and not getting hung up on semantics is to recognize the varying measures and degrees of God's Presence.

This is illustrated in Isaiah 6:1. The perplexing but wonderful truth about God manifesting His Presence is that when He shows up, there is more to come simply because of who He is and how big He is. It is very important to hunger for and invite the increase of His Presence.

When we read about the train of God's robe filling the temple, the word *filling* actually implies that His robe both filled the temple and continued to fill it. He came, but He kept coming, unveiling the reality that there is always more of Him to be experienced.

Even though we live filled with the Holy Spirit's Presence, there is more Presence available to us, not for receipt, but for experience and release. You and I received the same Holy Spirit as Jesus Christ. This Spirit is not inferior, nor is He a downgrade from the original model. Although it sounds humorous, there are many believers convinced that they are inaccessible to what Jesus had because *that was Jesus!* Jesus is forever unparalleled and unique in His role as Messiah; but He never intended to be unique when it came to His earthly works (unique as in the *only* one who healed the sick, performed the miraculous, set people free from torment, etc.). The same Spirit belongs to you and me; and when we experience powerful encounters in His Presence, it awakens us to what we possess and gives us the supernatural ability to release it to the world around us.

---

* Daily Reading: *HTP*, Pages 98-100

* Daily Scriptures: Isaiah 6, See below for remaining Scriptures

QUESTIONS:

1. Identify how God reveals His Presence in the following Scriptures:

   a. Colossians 1:17

   _____

   _____

   b. 1 Corinthians 6:19

   _____

   _____

c. Matthew 18:20

_____

_____

d. Psalm 22:3 (KJV)

_____

_____

e. 1 Kings 8:10-11

_____

_____

2. Write down three instances where you experienced God's Presence in unique ways. (Even though He lives inside of us, He still comes and encounters us in powerful and often tangible ways!)

a. _____

_____

b. _____

_____

c. _____

_____

Day 4

THE CRY FOR MORE

And when they had prayed, the place where they were assembled together was shaken; and they were all filled with the Holy Spirit, and they spoke the word of God with boldness.

—ACTS 4:31

This section of our study continues to build on itself. We just explored how it is actually legal for us to desire *more* of God's Presence and power as we recognize that we are not asking to get more. Rather, we want to be used as catalysts who experience and release the more that we have *already* received in the Holy Spirit. Now, let us look at what happens when we encounter the *more* of God and what we are supposed to do with it.

Did the apostles need an upgraded Holy Spirit? Absolutely not. The One they received on the Day of Pentecost was God, and there is no higher up you can go from there. So what happened in Acts 4 after they prayed for God to demonstrate His power through signs and wonders? The text says that the place was shaken, "and they were all filled with the Holy Spirit, and they spoke the word of God with boldness" (Acts 4:31).

Since they had already been filled with the Spirit's power, what was happening on this occasion? They were experiencing a new dimension of what they were already filled with. The Spirit came in power and literally shook the building where they were assembled. These powerful manifestations of the Holy Spirit are purposed to equip us with an encounter. Notice I used the word "equip." People often talk about "having" an encounter. That is great, so long as we steward that encounter well.

We must understand that we are equipped with encounters with the *more* of God, just like the apostles were in Acts 4, for a purpose. For them, it was to declare the Word of God with even greater boldness and effectiveness. For you and me, it is to impact whatever sphere of life the Lord has placed us in with His Kingdom purposes.

- Daily Reading: *HTP*, Pages 108-109

- Daily Scripture: Acts 4:23-31

QUESTIONS:

1. Why is it important to experience fresh encounters with the Holy Spirit in our lives? (It must be important since the early Church needed a fresh filling with the Holy Spirit in Acts 4:23-31.)

_____

_____

_____

_____

2. As a believer who is filled with the Holy Spirit, list some significant moments where you would say that you received a "fresh filling" with the Holy Spirit in your life:

a. ....

_____

b. ....

_____

c. ....

_____

3. What is the unique sphere of influence the Lord has called you to for this season? (Note: Basically, what stage of life are you currently in: Student, parent, business owner, arts and entertainment, retiree, etc.)

....

....

....

....

4. Practically speaking—how can you release God's Kingdom purposes in your current place in life? (For example: a church leader creating a revival culture, operating a business using Kingdom principles, raising your children up to treasure God's Presence, co-workers that you can pray for, starting a prayer group on campus, etc. *Be creative and seek the Lord on this!*)

....

....

....

....

Day 5

---❧---

THE CRY FOR OUTPOURING

"And I will not hide My face from them anymore; for I shall have poured out My Spirit on the house of Israel," says the Lord God.

—EZEKIEL 39:29

When it comes to living out the experience of our baptism in the Holy Spirit and immersion into His Presence, we must be careful not to get swept up into spiritual professionalism. Many people experience this glorious gift, and instead of embracing it as an invitation to greater intimacy and friendship with the Lord, it becomes a job promotion. Evangelist Reinhard Bonnke refers to this as the mistake of wearing our experience with the Holy Spirit as some type of spiritual "badge of honor."

Often, the outpouring of the Holy Spirit at Pentecost, and even the baptism of the Holy Spirit in the Church today, is emphasized for the supernatural increase of ministry effectiveness it produces. This is absolutely true. However, we should not seek this experience simply because of the greater effectiveness it brings to our ministry. This is a byproduct that we should expect, yes, but our paramount desire should be the *face-to-face* encounter it ushers us into with God.

In Ezekiel 39:29, the Lord describes a clear relationship between the outpouring of His Spirit and His people beholding His face—knowing Him in a greater, deeper way. Truth be told, the revelation of the face of God through the outpouring of the Spirit is made available to everyone. Wherever we go in revival, we cannot go past His face. It is easy to get distracted by demonstrations of power and manifestations. Signs and wonders can even become the end-all of revival. These things are truly our treasure and delight, not as an end in themselves, but because they all release greater glimpses of the Father's face and His divine nature.

We are most effective when our driving pursuit is intimacy with God. The moment our lives become ministry-driven or calling-driven rather than Presence-driven, we compromise our effectiveness and surrender the only thing of substance we truly have to offer the world: Him!

- Daily Reading: *HTP*, Pages 109-111

- Daily Scriptures: Ezekiel 39:29, Proverbs 16:15

QUESTIONS:

1. What have you been taught about the baptism of the Holy Spirit?

_____

_____

_____

_____

2. If you have experienced the baptism of the Holy Spirit, how has it specifically transformed your personal relationship with the Lord?

    a. ....

    b. ....

    c. ....

    d. ....

3. Read Proverbs 16:15. How does this verse link God's face and favor with the outpouring of His Spirit?

    ....

    ....

    ....

    ....

    ....

THE PROTOTYPE FOR NORMAL CHRISTIANITY

The Tabernacle of David is an Old Testament prototype for what the New Testament Church should look and function like. In David's Tabernacle, there were priests, praise, and Presence. The same should characterize the modern Body of Christ. Every believer is a priest with the ability to praise who has the potential to access and release God's Presence—individually, corporately, congregationally, regionally, and even globally!

"The Presence of the Lord was never meant to rest on something man creates."

—BILL JOHNSON

VIDEO GUIDE

1. The Presence of the Lord was never meant to rest on something man _____.

2. The Presence of God rests on _____, not ministries.

3. The Tabernacle of David is the _____ for the New Testament Church.

4. David danced _____ the Presence, not after.

5. Worship appears _____ to those not participating in it.

Day 1

WHAT HAPPENS WHEN THE WORLD STARTS COMING IN?

Go out into the highways and the hedges, and compel them to come in, so that my house may be filled.

—Luke 14:23

We must put hands and feet to what we believe when it comes to the lost, broken, and hurting people being found by the Master. Revival is messy. It's just how it is. The collision between His Presence and sinners is often dramatic, producing some unusual and uncomfortable things. While the unusual and uncomfortable should never become a distraction, we must be aware of what we are welcoming when we profess the desire to disciple nations and see cities saved. We need to ask ourselves, "Are we really sure about this?" And then, we need to count the cost. I pray that in light of *what* we offer, the so-called cost is tossed to the side. Remember, you receive an encounter to *be* an encounter.

In the context of the parable Jesus shares in Luke 14, there was some "messes" that responded to the summons and showed up at the house. In fact, all of the people who would be considered the clean, the prim and proper of society, the religious and spiritually "put together," were the very ones who made excuses when the invitation was extended for them to dine with the master of the house.

The result? "...Then the master of the house, being angry, said to his servant, 'Go out quickly into the streets and lanes of the city, and bring in here the poor and the maimed and the lame and the blind'" (Luke 14:21). This reality challenges all of us, as these are the very people whose conditions, maladies, and lifestyles are elements that set them up for life-changing encounters with God. These are the people God is calling to His family, as these were the people we were before we received the King's summons and accepted the invitation.

Let's bring this into our daily lives. The Lord will connect us with people who, for all intents and purposes, need a lot of help. Everything about them is messy and broken. And yet, the very fact that you—one marked by and filled with God's Presence—have crossed their path points to the strong likelihood of a supernatural setup. Be ready!

---

* Daily Reading: *HTP*, Pages 114-116

* Daily Scripture: Luke 14:16-24

QUESTIONS:

1. Read Luke 14:16-24. How would the people that the master ends up inviting to the party potentially cause a "problem," or be broken?

---

2. Honestly evaluate your own life and ministry. Have you avoided broken people and messy situations in favor of sticking with the comfortable and safe?

If so, *how* can you step beyond your comfort zone, and *who* can you start ministering to?

Day 2

GOD'S HOUSE—OLD TESTAMENT STYLE

...which are a shadow of things to come, but the substance is of Christ.

—COLOSSIANS 2:17

We look to the shadows and pictures presented in the Old Testament, as they give clarity to what we have received in substance. The Old Testament "houses" of God are very relevant, for they are pictures of what would be fulfilled through Jesus, and would ultimately be expressed through people such as you and me.

The five examples of God's house we observe in the Old Testament are as follows:

First, in Genesis 28, we read about Jacob's vision of the ladder to heaven. There was no building, but God's Presence was there. This is what made it *His* house!

Second, there is the Tabernacle of Moses, which gave us a prophetic portrait of Jesus. Every piece of furniture spoke of the coming Messiah. It was built according to the specific details God gave Moses in a face-to-face meeting on Mount Sinai.

Third, there is the Temple of Solomon. This was the most glorious and beautiful structure on the planet at the time. It represented humanity's best effort to host God's Presence and to house Him in a structure that was consistent with His worth.

Fourth, there is the restored Temple of Solomon. This was built to twice the size of the original, demonstrating the heart of God to restore things to greater places than they were before the restoration was needed. However, it did not contain the beauty that the former temple possessed.

Finally, there is the Tabernacle of David. This was built for worship. The Ark of the Covenant was there. The priests were there. And the Presence was there. God was present in His glory and the priests ministered to Him nonstop, day after day, night after night.

---

* Daily Reading: *HTP*, Pages 118-121

* Daily Scriptures: Amos 9:11-12, Acts 15:17, 1 Peter 2:5

QUESTIONS:

1. Read Amos 9:11-12 and Acts 15:17. Based on what you read in these verses, what will happen once David's Tabernacle is restored? (How would this affect people across the earth?)

_____

_____

_____

_____

2. Read First Peter 2:5. Compare what you read beside the description of David's Tabernacle and the priests who minister continuously before the Lord. How does the restoration of David's Tabernacle describe the day in which we are living?

----

3. Based on what you read about the five Old Testament houses of God, how can some of their characteristics apply to you today (as someone who actually *is* God's house)?

Day 3

THE PRESENCE AND THE PRIESTS

Then David said, "No one may carry the ark of God but the Levites, for the Lord has chosen them to carry the ark of God and to minister before Him forever."

—1 Chronicles 15:2

One of the most intriguing accounts in the Old Testament has to be when King David and his men were preparing to move the Ark of the Covenant into Jerusalem. David made arrangements to place it in the tent that he had pitched for that purpose. This was David's number one priority, as hosting God's Presence was this king's paramount pursuit.

The problem was due to a misunderstanding of the prototype that God was establishing, even in a time *before its time*. In other words, God wanted to release a glimpse of grace and New Testament practice while history was still under the Old Covenant and system.

Israel had planned for this incredible day! They lined the streets to witness the symphony of worship that was orchestrated to usher God's Presence into the City of David. The finest oxcart was obtained for the event. Priests took their places as they prepared for the Holy One's grand entry. Unfortunately, while en route, one of the oxen stumbled and nearly overturned the cart that carried the Ark.

Uzzah reached out his hand to steady the Ark, as he was concerned for the Presence. Despite his apparent good intentions, the anger of the Lord burned against Uzzah for his irreverence and the man was struck dead right there and then.

Principle? The Presence cannot be manhandled. Plus, we must be careful never to fit God's Presence into a mechanism fashioned by man. God will not ride on our oxcarts. In fact, His Presence will not rest on anything that we make—organizations, buildings, ministries, etc. They are good things, but the key is in recognizing His true resting place. God's Presence was always meant to be carried on the shoulders of the Levites (priests). Because of Jesus' blood, you and I are those priests! He lives within us and rests upon us.

- Daily Reading: *HTP*, Pages 121-124

- Daily Scriptures: 2 Samuel 6:1-11, 1 Chronicles 15:1-2, 1 Peter 2:4-10

QUESTIONS:

1. Read Second Samuel 6:1-11. How does the situation that happened with Uzzah point us toward God's plan for how His Presence *should* be properly carried?

_____

_____

_____

_____

2. Read First Chronicles 15:1-2. Who were the people designated to carry/move the Ark of the Covenant?

_____

_____

_____

_____

3. Read First Peter 2:4-10. Because of Jesus' blood and work on the Cross, you are a priest before the Lord. What does this mean to you in relation to carrying God's Presence?

_____

_____

_____

_____

Day 4

PERFECT THEOLOGY, PERFECT PROTOTYPE

Most assuredly, I say to you, he who believes in Me, the works that I do he will do also; and greater works than these he will do, because I go to My Father.

—John 14:12

Now that we recognize the prototypes and models that were given to us in the Old Testament (through buildings, the priesthood, etc.), it is time for us to examine the *ultimate prototype*: Jesus.

No man modeled hosting the Presence of God more effectively than the Son of Man. His very title, Jesus the *Christ*, points to His identity as the Anointed One. Because of the Holy Spirit, we all have the joy and privilege to partake of the anointing He modeled.

We are not discussing Jesus' identity as Messiah here. That is unparalleled, and there is nothing about His identity as Savior that mankind can model. He was the Messiah because God knew that we could never be able to do it. Regardless of how much of the law we tried to follow and how much good we tried to do, it all fell horribly flat, as our hearts were still rebellious in nature. We needed everything Jesus provided as Messiah and Savior of the world. There is none like the glorious, spotless Lamb of God.

That said, He is both Messiah *and* our model. Jesus Christ is our perfect sacrifice and He is perfect theology. His identity as the Christ refers to His anointing by the Holy Spirit. Want to know who God is and what He is like? Look at the Son. He is the standard, for both revealing the Father and for us to follow in living out the Christian life.

I'm jealous for what was upon and released through this Man, Jesus. Since I have discovered that Jesus lived life in a way that we could actually follow, I have found myself burning for the many things that came naturally to Him. They came naturally not because He was God, but because He was anointed by the Spirit. It is important that when we read the Gospels, we pay close attention to His works. Why? John 14:12—what He did, we are expected to do because we received the same indwelling Spirit!

---

* Daily Reading: *HTP*, Pages 131-136

* Daily Scripture: John 14:12-14

QUESTIONS:

1. What does the statement, "Jesus Christ is perfect theology," mean to you?

---

2. Explain what the following truths about Jesus mean to you:

a. Jesus is my Messiah:

_____

_____

_____

_____

b. Jesus is my model:

_____

_____

_____

_____

3. List some of the miracles that you have seen happen by your own hands, anointed by the Holy Spirit (example: healing, leading someone to the Lord, seeing someone set free from torment, moving in the gifts of the Holy Spirit, etc.).

a. _____

b. _____

c. _____

d. _____

Day 5

---⟡---

LIVING WITH THE DOVE IN MIND

And John bore witness, saying, "I saw the Spirit descending from heaven like a dove, and He remained upon Him."

—JOHN 1:32

Jesus Christ is not only perfect theology, revealing who the Father is, and He is not only our perfect model, showing what the normal Christian life should look like, but He is the ultimate prototype for what it means to host the Presence of God. The Spirit of God was able to come upon Him and *remain* for one major reason: He was without sin. Because of the blood Jesus shed at the Cross, we have been qualified to enjoy the same experience with the Holy Spirit, as His blood has washed away all our sin…forever!

In the accounts of Jesus' water baptism and subsequent baptism in the Holy Spirit, we see the Spirit of God descending on Him *like a dove.* We need to examine this process carefully, as misunderstanding can lead to all types of confusion.

The Holy Spirit is a person, not a dove. His resting upon Jesus is compared to a dove. When we start seeing the Spirit as a dove, He quickly goes from being a He to an "it." As we all know, it is one thing to

139

have a relationship with a friend who is a "he or she," but it is another thing to attempt to engage your automobile or bicycle in relationship. Again, friends are people while the latter items are things—"its"!

We know that the Holy Spirit lives in every born-again believer. The sad reality is that He does not rest *upon* every believer. He lives inside of me for my sake, but He rests upon me for the sake of the world.

I often ask people what they would do if an actual dove landed on their shoulders. How would they walk around a room, or go about their day? A common answer is, "Carefully." That's a good answer, but not good enough. There is religion in that response, as our works are the primary focus. The right answer is, "Every step is with the dove in mind." It's not about being hyperaware of our actions, but it's rather about being aware of the One who rests upon us.

---

* Daily Reading: *HTP*, Pages 136-137

* Daily Scripture: John 1:32-34

QUESTIONS:

1. What are some ways you can live mindful of the Holy Spirit's Presence?

_____

_____

_____

_____

2. What is the difference between being focused on our actions and being focused on a person (the Holy Spirit)?

_____

_____

_____

3. Bill Johnson makes the statement, "He lives inside me for my sake, but He rests upon me for your sake," referring to the Holy Spirit. How does the Presence of the Holy Spirit resting *upon* you benefit other people?

_____

_____

_____

_____

KEYS TO PRACTICALLY RELEASING GOD'S PRESENCE

The key is not becoming overly focused on the specific method of releasing God's Presence—whether it would be through decree, prophetic acts, faith, anointed cloths, etc. The focus must always be the Presence of God that empowers the method, as methods are subject to change, even on a situational basis. In fact, God will most likely take you on an adventure to discover new, potentially unusual methods of releasing His Presence. If the focus is always Him, however, then there is always room to be adventurous in the methods—just as long as they do not distract from His Presence, His work, and His Word.

"Many times breakthrough does not only come through instruction; it comes through adventure."
—BILL JOHNSON

VIDEO GUIDE

1. This breakthrough did not come through instruction; it came through _____.

2. Your shadow will always release what _____ you.

3. The dove is always looking for a place to _____.

4. The Holy Spirit lives inside of us for our sake; but He is upon us for _____ else.

5. The Kingdom of God is _____ the Holy Spirit.

6. Ways to release God's Presence:

   a. _____.

   b. _____.

   c. The _____ act.

   d. Act of _____.

Day 1

POWER AND AUTHORITY

And Jesus came and spoke to them, saying, "All authority has been given to Me in heaven and on earth. Go therefore and make disciples of all the nations…"

—Matthew 28:18-19

Jesus had given His disciples a measure of power and authority during a period of time while He was still on the earth. However, this experience was temporary, special, and unsustainable. Why? Because the empowering Presence had not yet been poured out through the Holy Spirit. What Jesus was doing with His disciples was purposed to further establish a model.

Even though we are starting to really go after this understanding of Jesus as our model for the normal, supernatural Christian life, there is still a barrier that thwarts many Christians from crossing over into the territory of living the actual Jesus lifestyle. This barrier is the thought, *Well, that was Jesus—the Son of God. And I am not Jesus!*

The Gospels and the Book of Acts are very intentional in showing us the model of Jesus being expressed through other anointed people—apostle and non-apostle alike! The key is in understanding encounter and commission, power and authority. What is the relationship between these? Our encounters with God are always meant to bless and renew us personally, but they are also designed to serve as a reminder of what authority authorizes us to bring to others.

I liken it to waves. When God's power manifests—either sovereignly, or released in a meeting, through a person, or in an environment—those of us in the "splash zone" ride the wave that His power creates. It does not take much. Basically, the only prerequisite is proximity. If we are in an atmosphere where His power is released, we ride the wave and encounter God dynamically.

These encounters with God are incredible. However, I want to share a secret with you that empowers you to live life "between encounters" and helps you release those waves of power to others. The secret? It is simply, authority. What you experience while riding a wave of His power, you have received the authority to release anytime through Jesus' commission.

---

* Daily Reading: *HTP*, Pages 161-162

* Daily Scriptures: Matthew 28:18-19, Luke 24:49, Acts 1:1-8

QUESTIONS:

1. Read Acts 1:1-8. How does receiving the Holy Spirit empower you for ministry?

_____

_____

_____

_____

2. Describe your understanding of power and authority, and how they work together in your life.

_____

3.   What does it mean to learn how to "live life between encounters?"

Day 2

INTENTIONALLY RELEASING GOD'S PRESENCE...THROUGH WORDS

The words that I speak to you are spirit, and they are life.

—John 6:63b

Everything Jesus said and did was empowered by the Holy Spirit. This includes the very words He spoke. When we are speaking under the influence of the same Holy Spirit, we can expect the same release of spirit and life that Jesus experienced. This is one of four ways that we can release God's Presence in an intentional manner.

Jesus used words quite frequently in His ministry to release the supernatural. This begs the question: What empowered His words? He only said what His Father was saying, which meant that every word He spoke had its origins in the heart of the Father. It is difficult for us to imagine the relationship that God enjoyed *with God* through the exchange between the Son and the Father. Nevertheless, Jesus would often retreat to be alone with the Father. It had to be during these moments of intimacy where He was exposed to the Father's heart, heard what He was saying, and saw what He was doing.

This same intimacy positions you and me to declare words that release worlds. When we discern what the Father is saying, and speak His very words, His world and Kingdom is established in our midst. Those words from the Father's heart carry the Presence, which releases God's world into this one. Powerful.

Have you ever been in a situation where there was an air of turmoil or unrest, and someone, simply by speaking, released peace into the situation and completely transformed the atmosphere? That is exactly what you and I are being called to do through our words. By saying what the Father is saying, we actually release the creative nature and Presence of God into a situation to bring His influence and change.

- Daily Reading: *HTP*, Pages 163-164

- Daily Scriptures: John 6:63-68, John 8:28, John 8:38, John 12:49-50, John 14:10

QUESTIONS:

1. Describe a time in your life where someone's words literally changed the situation or atmosphere.

_____

_____

_____

_____

2. How are you supposed to do the same thing through your words?

_____

_____

_____

3. Read the following verses: John 8:28, John 8:38, John 12:49-50, and John 14:10. What does it mean to *say what the Father is saying*?

_____

_____

_____

_____

Day 3

INTENTIONALLY RELEASING GOD'S PRESENCE...THROUGH ACTIONS

Then Jesus answered and said to them, "Most assuredly, I say to you, the Son can do nothing of Himself, but what He sees the Father do; for whatever He does, the Son also does in like manner."

—JOHN 5:19

Yet again, Jesus is our model here. He spoke the Father's words and did the Father's works. We must have eyes open to see what the Father is doing, how He wants to move, and be willing to jump right into the action—*however* He wants to use us. Henry Blackaby, author of *Experiencing God*, refers to this as us moving where God is blessing.

To intentionally release God's Presence through certain actions, we need to truly grasp this revelation of authority. We are able to actually step out and bring God's Presence into a situation through certain actions because of our identity. Jesus authorized us to do this. The Holy Spirit is the only "credential" you need. Again, keep your eyes open for places the Father is working, and have a heart willing to yield to the Spirit's leading.

Here are three intentional ways you can release God's Presence through actions:

Act of faith: If you are the one receiving a healing, for example, I would encourage you to try to do something you could not do while you were sick (use wisdom, of course). If you are the one administering healing, make the same request of the person you are praying for. We read how Jesus *saw their faith* and released His power.

The prophetic act: Jesus operated in this many times. For example, He instructed a blind man to go wash in the pool of Siloam (see John 9:7). The pool did not contain miracle water. Rather, it was the blind man's prophetic act that released the miracle.

Touch: One of the foundational doctrines of the Church is the "laying on of hands" (see Heb. 6:1-2). Laying hands on people is a tool that God uses to release the authority of His world and His Presence upon another. It brings healing, impartation, deliverance, commissioning, etc.

*   Daily Reading: *HTP*, Pages 164-165

*   Daily Scriptures: John 9:1-13, Hebrews 6:1-2

QUESTIONS:

1. Can you think of three occasions in the Gospels where Jesus exhibits these intentional ways of releasing God's Presence?

    a. Act of faith _____

    _____

    _____

    b. The prophetic act _____

c. Touch

2. How has God used each of these intentional methods in your own life?

a. Act of faith

b. The prophetic act

c. Touch

Day 4

---※---

UNINTENTIONAL WAYS OF RELEASING HIS PRESENCE

...so that they brought the sick out into the streets and laid them on beds and couches, that at least the shadow of Peter passing by might fall on some of them.

—Acts 5:15

We have explored some intentional ways of releasing God's Presence. There are also some ways of releasing God's Presence that are unintentional on our part and are the byproduct of His Presence overshadowing our lives. These unintentional releases of God's Presence are often exciting and fun to experience, as they continue to demolish any type of box that we attempt to put Him in.

Shadow: One of the best illustrations of unintentional ways of releasing God's Presence is the account in Acts 5:15, where we read about Peter's shadow releasing healing power. There were no classes or seminars on how to activate an anointed shadow. There was no sermon series on the ten steps to releasing breakthrough with your shadow. The point? The methods will often change, so it is important that we are flexible with how God wants to use us. The key is always being Presence-driven. Remember, your shadow will always release what overshadows you.

Compassion: This is not an act, but it is a posture of the heart—hence, why it is in the unintentional category. Jesus released Presence and power, time after time, because He was moved by compassion. It was just who He was. When we live the Jesus-modeled life, compassion becomes part of our spiritual DNA. Being willing to love people with the love of Christ brings the miraculous to the forefront. God's sovereignty has little to do with the multitude of miracles people experience on the mission field. I believe it has everything to do with compassion colliding with desperation.

Clothing: The Presence upon clothing operates through the same principle as the shadow mentioned above. We see this present on both Jesus and Paul. When people touched Jesus' garment, power flowed out of Him and brought healing. The same was true with Paul and handkerchiefs that he touched and gave to those who were sick. Does this mean we create a theology out of anointed clothing? No. It has little to do with *what* type of vessel is releasing the Presence, and everything to do with the One whose Presence is being released. Clothing is unimportant; it's faith in the Presence that releases anointing..

* Daily Reading: *HTP*, Pages 165-166

* Daily Scriptures: Acts 5:12-16, Mark 1:40-42, Acts 19:11-12

QUESTIONS:

1. What does "unintentionally releasing God's Presence" mean to you, and what does it look like?

2. Have you experienced any of these three examples of unintentionally releasing God's Presence? If so, share one or two testimonies of how you witnessed an unintentional release of God's Presence in your life:

a. ....

....

....

b. ....

....

....

3. Can you think of some other ways (not mentioned above), in your life, church, or experience with the Lord, where you have seen God's Presence and power released in an unintentional way (in other words, where He powerfully moved and no one was trying to make anything happen)?

....

....

....

....

Day 5

WORSHIP THAT CHARGES
THE ATMOSPHERE

...we hear them speaking in our own tongues the wonderful works of God.

—Acts 2:11

Worship that is God-centered releases His Presence and transforms the atmosphere. We do not worship the Lord to *get* something. If there is anything we are looking to obtain in the worship experience, it is *Him*. Period. Remember, this is an unintentional method of releasing His Presence.

I classify worship in the "unintentional" category for good reason. Worship is not our equation to receive breakthrough or blessing. At the same time, when we authentically and extravagantly lavish Him with the praise He so deserves, He cannot help but inhabit our praise and invade the environment. And of course, we know what happens when *He* comes.

One of the reasons that the atmosphere was charged with God's Presence on the Day of Pentecost was because of worship. Such praise, "speaking...the wonderful works of God," contributed to a significant atmospheric shift over an entire city. This confronted and broke spiritual blindness, and helped usher 3,000 souls into the Kingdom.

I've seen this for myself when we've rented out a particular facility for church services, only to have the people who used it afterward comment on the Presence that lingers. A friend of mine used to take people onto the streets of San Francisco many years ago. They were met with heavy resistance. But when he realized that when God arises, His enemies are scattered, he strategically used this approach for ministry (see Ps. 68). He split his team into two. One half went out to worship, and the other half would minister to people. The police told him that when he is on the streets, crime stops. This is an amazing result from the Presence being released over a part of the city through praise. The atmosphere changes as the Presence is given rightful place.

---

* Daily Reading: *HTP*, Pages 166-167

* Daily Scriptures: Acts 2:5-12, Psalm 68

QUESTIONS:

1. How does worship release God's Presence in an unintentional way? Why is worship unintentional instead of intentional?

2. In what ways does worship impact the atmosphere?

_____

_____

3. Think of a time in your life where you experienced praise and worship that impacted the atmosphere. Describe how God's Presence was released and what happened.

_____

_____

_____

_____

Session 8

YOUR BAPTISM OF FIRE

Testimony is prophetic. When someone shares his or her encounter with God, it releases an invitation for every person within hearing distance to hunger for what that person experienced. God is intensely personal, so we should not expect the identical encounter as someone else had. They are all dramatic; whether someone experiences something physically electrifying, or through a still small voice, they receive a word that goes onto define the way they do life and ministry.

"Authority comes in the commission; power comes in the encounter."

—Bill Johnson

Day 1

THE POWER OF TESTIMONY

...For the testimony of Jesus is the spirit of prophecy.

—REVELATION 19:10

As we finish up our time together, I want to look at some people throughout history who embraced the assignment to host God's Presence with their lives and ministries. However, before we focus on these stories, it is important that we understand why we share testimonies to begin with.

To some reading these incredible accounts of what God did through yielded men and women, they are simply nice stories. I am not satisfied with a story that does take me into a greater revelation of God's nature *and* that does not position people in the here and now to encounter His current Presence from that previous breakthrough.

Whether the testimony is a thousand years old or a minute old, if it accurately reveals the nature and character of God, it contains the potential to release His Presence. In addition, by sharing what the Lord has done, we are actually setting our audience up to experience Him in that same way. He is no respecter of persons. What He did for one person, He will do for another. What He did in the days of the apostles, He will do today. He is unchanging, and longs to reveal who He is through His supernatural activity.

Testimony carries Presence. When you share a testimony of something impossible that had to bend its knee to the supremacy of Jesus and the authority of His name, God's Presence is actually released and possesses the potential to stir faith in those listening to you share.

We must properly understand testimony if we truly want the following information to be applicable to those of us living in the twenty-first century. D.L. Moody, Evan Roberts, and Charles Finney are no longer on the earth. However, their lives still possess relevance for us if we accept the invitation their testimonies and stories present. How do we accept this invitation through past accounts? We hear what God did to and through these people and respond accordingly: "Lord, do it again—here I am, use me!"

These testimonies unveil what is possible to anyone willing to embrace the assignment and host His Presence!

———————————— ❧ ————————————

* Daily Reading: *None*

* Daily Scriptures: Revelation 19:10, Psalm 78:1-8

QUESTIONS:

1. Read Revelation 19:10. How does testimony of what Jesus has done minister prophetically?

2. Have you ever shared a testimony and watched God use it in a powerful way? If so, describe your experience.

_____

_____

_____

_____

If you've witnessed this happen with someone else (but not in your own life), describe that experience.

_____

_____

_____

_____

3. Read Psalm 78:1-8. Why do you think the testimony was so important to the Israelites?

_____

_____

_____

_____

Day 2

BUILDING YOUR PERSONAL
HISTORY WITH GOD

I can lay hands on you and impart an anointing into your life as God wills. But I can't give you my history with God.

—BILL JOHNSON

I want to take the next few moments to encourage you. As you read the stories and testimonies in the days to come, refuse to remain at a distance. You are not a spectator looking back from the twenty-first century. If these were *just* stories and if it were *only* history, spectatorship would be allowable. However, these testimonies are alive because they give real expression to the written Word. In other words, what is written in Scripture is given tangibility and substance when someone actually experiences the written in real-life form!

This is why it is important to study the lives and exploits of those who have gone before us. Since they were anointed by the same Spirit that lives inside of you and me, their history is actually part of our history with God. We are not memorializing the "good ole days" or setting up monuments to any person.

Rather, we honor the Presence that these men and women hosted and receive encouragement that if God released such power through their lives, He can surely do the same through you and me.

The key is recognizing the personal, individual nature of developing this history with God. I can lay hands on you and impart an anointing into your life as God wills. But I can't give you my history with God. This is developed between you and the Lord, and one of the ways this happens is through the cultivation of hunger in the secret place. You catch a glimpse of a testimony, either in the Scripture or in Church history, witnessing the grace and power that the "extraordinary" heroes of the faith moved in, and your natural response is, "Lord, I want that!"

After all, the so-called "extraordinary" heroes of Scripture were all very ordinary. What added the "extra" to their ordinary was the grace of His Presence, empowering them to do the impossible and shape history.

As we get ready to observe a few snapshots from history, remember that everything you read about is accessible to you. In fact, the potential to do what you read about lives inside of you! This is not New Age philosophy or positive thinking. The power source is the Spirit of God. You did not receive a second-class Holy Spirit compared to the "great" heroes of the faith, both in the early Church and throughout Church history. It is essential that you build testimonies of past breakthrough—both your own and those from other believers—into your personal history with God. Why? They are markers that unceasingly remind you of what is accessible when normal men and women embrace the assignment to host His Presence.

- Daily Reading: *HTP*, Pages 179-181

- Daily Scripture: *None*

PRAYER ASSIGNMENT:

Spend some time in prayer today, preparing your heart for what the Holy Spirit will be revealing to you over the next few days. Rather than answering questions after the following entries, I am going to ask you to use some brief prayers as launch pads for your personal prayer time.

Let's start off by praying together:

Father, I thank You for the gift of Your Presence living inside of me.

I am so grateful that the same Spirit that raised Jesus from the dead lives within me, and empowers me to bring Your Kingdom on earth as it is in heaven.

Lord, prepare my heart to taste and hunger. Your Word says to "taste and see that You are good" (see Ps. 34:8).

In Your Kingdom, to eat is to increase in hunger. As I feed on testimonies of what You have done through anointed men and women throughout history, I am not watching their lives as an observer or spectator. What they enjoyed, what they released, what they experienced, and how they shaped history—that same Spirit lives inside of me and has given me the same possibilities that were available to the great heroes of the faith.

Their history belongs to me because we all have received the same Holy Spirit, the same power, the same potential, and the same commission.

In Jesus' name, amen.

Day 3

EVAN ROBERTS AND THE WELSH REVIVAL

PERSISTING FOR THE PRESENCE

Ask, and it will be given to you; seek, and you will find; knock, and it will be opened to you. For everyone who asks receives, and he who seeks finds, and to him who knocks it will be opened.
—MATTHEW 7:7-8

William Davies, a deacon at the Moriah Chapel, encouraged young Evan Roberts never to miss the prayer meetings in case the Holy Spirit came and Evan was found missing.

Evan's attendance was not motivated by religion, form, or duty, but out of sheer hunger for a historic visitation of God's Presence. The expression of his hunger was seen in his faithful attendance of daily prayer meetings. He did this for 13 years, contending for a mighty visitation of the Holy Spirit. History records that Roberts got what he asked for.

Just because it took Evan Roberts 13 years before he actually saw the fruit of his prayers does not mean we ought to expect our prayers to come to fruition in the same time frame. It may take longer; but it may be exponentially faster. Ours is not the right to try to evaluate the "whys" of God's time frame. Rather, we are instructed to ask, and keep on asking. We are invited to seek with the expectation of finding. Not wish. Not maybe. Not "you never know with God." Jesus sets the model and establishes a protocol where the one asking, seeking, and knocking is commanded to expect something on the other side of his or her persistence.

What was on the other side of Roberts' 13 years of asking, seeking, and knocking? Historic revival that shifted the spiritual geography of the entire nation of Wales, set the stage for the Pentecostal outpouring at Azusa Street, and has left behind a lingering Presence of the Lord that can still be felt in Moriah Chapel.

Breakthroughs like Roberts' serve as examples for you and me. They remind us to follow Jesus' instructions to ask, seek, and knock, as we must have expectation that on the other side of our persistence will come breakthrough in due season. Specifically, Roberts was contending for an outpouring and release of God's Presence. While the principles for relentless, persistent asking are certainly applicable for any request we desire of the Lord, I pray that as we continue to experience His Presence and taste of His glory, our *one thing* will become obvious: *"Come with Your Presence, Lord!"*

---

* Daily Reading: *HTP*, Pages 192-194

* Daily Scripture: *None*

PRAYER ASSIGNMENT:

Lord, I ask, seek, and knock with the expectation that I will receive answers. The door will open, and I will find You.

You are good and I know You desire to heal, deliver, restore, provide, and answer. The things dear to my heart are also dear to Yours.

Above all, I desire to pursue and persist for Your Presence.

Now think of some areas in your life, church, community, or family, where you would like the Lord to release His Presence and bring supernatural transformation.

Pray for these specific requests, not with the answered prayer being your final desire, but for the release of His Presence and glory. There is no question as to whether or not He wants to answer your prayer—He does, as it is in agreement with His will, plan and good purpose. However, let's make it our goal to become lovers of His Presence and people who learn how to usher Him in. This sets us up for consistent victory.

Day 4

CHARLES FINNEY

A WALKING REVIVAL

Or do you not know that your body is a temple of the Holy Spirit who is in you...
—1 CORINTHIANS 6:19

When history remembers Charles Finney, there are two sides of his ministry that deserve our focus. The first, of course, are the powerful revival services where Finney preached with incredible efficacy, witnessing mass conversions to Christ.

However, the key to Finney's power in the pulpit is tied to what we observe on a smaller scale in his personal life and one-on-one ministry. Not only did he sow into creating a revival climate in large gatherings and services, but it seems like he was ever mindful of Who he carried, and faithfully lived every step with "the dove in mind." In other words, Finney released the Presence and power of revival in his everyday life, just as he did in the historic gatherings.

As a result, we read about the historic supernatural encounters Finney had in both experiencing and releasing God's Presence. On one occasion that he notes in his autobiography, he entered a factory where young ladies were working on their weaving machines, looms, and spinning devices. Two of these women stood out to him. They looked a bit agitated, but tried to cover it up with laughter.

Finney approached closer and noticed that one was trembling so badly that she could not mend her thread. When he got about eight to ten feet away, they burst out in tears and slumped down. Within moments, the whole roomful of workers was in tears. The owner, an unbeliever at the time, recognized that this was a divine moment and ordered that his factory be shut down to give his workers a chance to come to Christ. A mini-revival broke out, which lasted several days. Nearly the entire mill was converted during this time.

What produced such a powerful atmosphere? It's simple: Finney was a man upon whom the Spirit of God loved to rest. Was Finney a special case? Did God like him more than other people? Are we called to look back upon the lives of revivalists like him and think to ourselves, "Well, that was Charles Finney," memorializing the exploits performed because of the unique Presence upon his life? No. Charles Finney is an invitation to any believer hungry enough to steward the Presence of God in his or her own life.

---

* Daily Reading: *HTP*, Pages 200-201

* Daily Scripture: *None*

PRAYER ASSIGNMENT:

Lord, I accept the invitation that You are giving me through this testimony of Charles Finney. He was a normal person, just like me, who was filled with the same Holy Spirit who lives inside of me. Show me how to host Your Presence like he did.

May I be a walking, talking revival. Father, give me ears to hear what You are saying and eyes to see what You are doing.

Where Your Spirit is moving, may I be sensitive to cooperate.

Help me to step out in the authority given to me by Jesus and release Your Presence through boldness and risk.

Empower and embolden me to carry and release Your Presence wherever I go, in Jesus' name.

Day 5

THIS IS MY STORY…AND YOURS

In my personal quest for the increased power and Presence of the Lord in my ministry, I have traveled to many cities, including Toronto. God has used my experiences in such places to set me up for life-changing encounters at home.

Just a quick word of encouragement—never feel like you have missed out on God if you go to a highly charged environment where the Spirit of God is moving powerfully, and you do not have a *dramatic* encounter. Just because there is an absence of the dramatic does not mean there was no encounter.

While the dramatic is often wonderful, if not blatantly life-changing, many of the moments that have shaped my life and ministry in the most significant ways happened without much fanfare. The Presence of God would minister to me in profound, but deeply personal ways and my life would be forever changed.

As I shared this recently in an interview, the person leading the conversation commented, "Those moments would not make for a good movie." I had to laugh, as he was absolutely correct. No they would not. But again, it was those moments in His Presence and hearing His voice that changed everything for me, and ultimately, set me up for some extremely dramatic encounters down the road.

In the book *Hosting the Presence*, I share about the 3 A.M. encounter I had with God where His Presence touched me so powerfully, I wondered if I would ever function "normally" again. This dramatic encounter with His Presence was the response to a contending in my spirit. The prayer I had been praying for months prior to this experience was "God, I must have more of You at any cost."

This ultimately begs the question: *How can I experience more of God's Presence when I have already received the Holy Spirit?* Simple. You have received the fullness of God in the Holy Spirit. The question is, how much of the fullness are you experiencing and releasing in your life currently? The Holy Spirit is willing to give you the measure you will jealously guard. There is no lesser or downgraded Holy Spirit. When you receive the Spirit, you receive God. Period. The pursuit of *more* involves your becoming awakened to the reality that the Presence of God lives inside of you. The Presence we have been studying that dwelt in the Tabernacle, that was always meant to be carried and transported by God's priests, is the Presence that you have received.

Here is the challenge. This study is not intended to merely increase information, but everything was written and assembled to stir your hunger for *more*. I pray that you become more aware of the Presence of the Holy Spirit resting upon your life and that a relentless pursuit has been birthed within you to go after Him. Remember, you have been chosen to be His eternal dwelling place. You have been chosen to host His Presence!

WHAT NEXT?

Here are a few things I recommend that you do to continually stir your appetite for His Presence:

- *Study the Scriptures*, both Old and New Testaments, and focus on the people who encountered God's Presence in life-changing ways (Jacob, Moses, David, Paul, etc.). Read their stories until a cry is birthed within you to experience what they enjoyed, and not be satisfied until you begin to encounter God's Presence like they did. Remember, you are the heir of a new and better covenant. If those in the Old Testament experienced God's glory in powerful measures, how much more is that glory available to you under the blood of Jesus?

- *Feed on the testimonies.* We always begin with the Word, as it is foundational. However, I recommend that you complement your time in the Scripture by reading biographies of revivalists throughout history. One of my personal favorites is John G. Lake. Witnessing his life and ministry through his writings stirs my hunger to pursue what he had. God is no respecter of persons, so if He moved through John G. Lake, I have to believe that it is also available to me, and it is available to you!

- *Watch for what He is doing.* Let us constantly be on the lookout, in our churches, in our communities, in our nation, for the activity of His Presence. I have often said, "Follow signs and wonders until they start following you." The key is a heart bent toward Him and His Presence. If you hear of His authentic movement in an environment or place, going there must always be considered an investment. You are freely receiving so you can, in turn, freely give.

Answer Key

HOSTING THE PRESENCE

SESSION 1:

YOUR AUTHORITY TO RELEASE GOD'S PRESENCE

1. authority

2. sin

3. no

4. delegated

5. order

6. man

SESSION 2:

YOUR SIGNIFICANCE IN HIS PRESENCE

1. greater

2. agreement

3. empower

4. priests

5. Two ministries of priests:

   a. God

   b. people

6. Two ministries to people:

   a. believers

   b. world

7. become

8. acts

9. nature

10. sacrifice

SESSION 3:

EMPOWERED BY HIS PRESENCE

1. fear

2. weakness

3. uniqueness

SESSION 4:
A SNEAK PREVIEW OF GOD'S HOUSE

    1. The house of God has:

        a. Heaven

        b. Angelic

        c. voice

    2. transition

    3. two

    4. initial fulfillment

    5. before

SESSION 5:
THE ANSWER TO ANCIENT CRIES

    1. upon

    2. dove

    3. conscious

    4. responding

    5. possession, account

    6. face

SESSION 6:
THE PROTOTYPE FOR NORMAL CHRISTIANITY

    1. creates

    2. people

    3. prototype

    4. before

    5. foolish

SESSION 7:
KEYS TO PRACTICALLY RELEASING GOD'S PRESENCE

    1. adventure

    2. overshadows

    3. rest

    4. everyone

    5. in

    6. Ways to release God's Presence:

        a. Word

        b. Touch

        c. prophetic

        d. faith

SESSION 8:
YOUR BAPTISM OF FIRE

    (None)

LOOKING FOR MORE FROM BILL JOHNSON AND BETHEL CHURCH?

Purchase additional resources—CDs, DVDs, digital downloads, music—from Bill Johnson and the Bethel team at the Bethel store.

Visit www.bjm.org for more information on Bill Johnson, to view his speaking itinerary, or to look into additional teaching resources.

To order Bethel Church resources, visit http://store.ibethel.org

Subscribe to iBethel.TV to access the latest sermons, worship sets, and conferences from Bethel Church.

To subscribe, visit www.ibethel.tv

Become part of a Supernatural Culture that is transforming the world and apply to the Bethel School of Supernatural Ministry.

For more information, visit www.ibethel.org/school-of-ministry

51140687R00107

Made in the USA
Columbia, SC
13 February 2019